The Gentle Celebrant's Guide

Funerals For Children

By Veronika Sophia Robinson
Cover illustration by Sarah Esau

Published by Celebrant Collection,
an imprint of Starflower Press

Funerals for Children
Copyright Veronika Sophia Robinson
Copyright cover art by Sara Esau
Published by Celebrant Collection,
Starflower Press www.starflowerpress.com
Full Moon in Virgo, February 2024
ISBN: 978-1-7385324-0-7

This book has been written for our certified Heart-led Celebrants and our celebrants-in-training. The language used reflects that; however, it is hoped that celebrants who've trained, or are training, elsewhere, will also benefit.

Names and identifying features have been changed.

Dedication

For my unborn daughters:
Jessica
Anastasia
Sequoia
Isabella

Although you never breathed in the fresh air of this beautiful Earth or danced in the rain;

even though you never skipped through a field of wildflowers or felt the rush of a breeze through your hair;

and though you never felt the ache of laughing till your sides hurt, or knew the bliss of sunshine warming your skin, or ran barefoot on the beach, or slid down a slippery slide;

what I want you know is that you are more than a footnote in my life. I loved you then, and I love you now. Until we meet again, play amongst the stars. You'll always be my babies.

And for my beautiful daughters and granddaughter who do live and love on this Earth, you are magnificent!

For all children, both near and far.
Mine
Yours
Theirs.

May we love them.
May we honour them.
May we remember them.

When Lexie's baby died, less than a day after birth, Lexie and Lionel's world fell apart, as did the lives of their children Barry and Patricia. A week after the funeral, Lexie's mother-in-law said "Time to get back to normal now."

Fifteen years later, Lexie hasn't 'got over it'.

There is no 'normal' after your child has died.

Exploring Spaces

This book is about spaces. The space we, as celebrants, hold for others, the myriad spaces that a person inhabits when they experience the death of a child, the spaces children live and love in, and the spaces we, as celebrants, hold for ourselves.

For the purposes of this book, a child is defined from during pregnancy through to young adulthood.

A number of years ago, I had a woman come to me for celebrant training. As our training is on a one-to-one basis, we spend a lot of time getting to know potential certified celebrants, and help them to unravel biases, and learn more about themselves. We were only on day two of a five-day training when she started crying with frustration: "This is the hardest course I've ever done!" In that moment, I wondered if I should simply refund the student and send her on her merry little way. Of course it's hard! Working with the bereaved isn't a picnic. It is *sacred* work. A holy undertaking (whether you're of faith or no faith) whereby we walk on hallowed ground as Gatekeepers of the

Liminal Space and Guardians of the Threshold. It's not like we're sitting in the sunshine eating ice cream. We are companions and *people of presence* during the darkest days of a parent's life.

"Let's get out of here," I said to her, and we left my living room and went for a drive. We arrived at a small cemetery, and walked to the far end. There, beneath the shade of an old gnarled cypress tree, was a grave. As she stepped closer, and read the aging headstone, she saw it was for a little girl.

"Fifty years later, and someone is still bringing gifts to this grave. Fifty years," I repeated softly. "Can you imagine? That pain, the grief, the ache and emptiness is never ending." I let the words settle. "As a funeral celebrant, we are walking alongside someone/a family for a week or two, maybe longer depending on where your celebrant practice is geographically, but those parents, siblings, grandparents, aunties, uncles and cousins live with this for life. *This*," I said gently, "is why you're finding this training is so difficult. Our own heart *has* to be broken. You can't just walk in and out of people's grief stories like it's no different to packing shelves in a supermarket."

"Your pain is the breaking of the shell
that encloses your understanding."
- Khalil Gibran

Too many people come to funeral celebrancy as a way to make a 'quick buck' and to feel financially secure by choosing to be in a recession-proof business. As a celebrant trainer, I don't take on such people. If that is someone's motivation for becoming a funeral celebrant (and, the truth is, for a lot of people it *is* their motivation) then it makes the world a far poorer place.

What this book is, and what this book is not
The seeds for this book were planted years ago, and came about after hearing a male celebrant speak so disrespectfully about officiating at the service of a pre-term infant. "I've just officiated for a foetus!" he mocked as if the idea was ludicrous, the sound of his snort with me all these years later. As the mother of four babies who died before term, his words shook me to the core. How heartless. How uncaring. "Tell me again why you're a funeral celebrant? Oh, that's right: pocket money to add onto your fat police pension!" That's what I wanted to say. How dare someone like him be allowed anywhere near a grieving parent? And yet,

this type of celebrant does exist, and they're the voice for heartbroken parents.

This book is designed to have you quietly contemplating whether you are the right person for this role, and to consider how you hold yourself when with the bereaved. It was never my intention for this book to be a treatise on how to write a funeral for a child, and it offers no templates. Just as entering the world of grief is unknown territory for a parent/grandparent, so too is this area unknown for us. We may bring certain skills with us, but if we enter each experience with a sense of heightened awareness that we're crossing a sacred threshold then we'll never take the blasé attitude of that man who showed no respect nor exhibited any emotional intelligence.

This book is not intended as a how-to manual for writing funerals for children. Each child, and each family, requires different things from us. If you understand the purpose of ceremony, and the three stages: separation, transition and incorporation, then you'll know how to write a ceremonial script. You won't learn how to write a eulogy from this book (refer to *Write That Eulogy* for crafting that part of a script).

This book's purpose is to open your heart wide to the gut-wrenching grip grief has on the bereaved, and to ask yourself if you have the gentleness and capacity for silence so that another may find comfort in your presence. I don't believe the role of a celebrant is for those who like to 'be the centre of attention'. This applies even more so to that of officiating funerals for children.

Although this book was specifically written for people who are training or have trained with us as Heart-led Celebrants, if you're reading it, the chances are high that you're a funeral celebrant, celebrant-in-training, minister, vicar or priest seeking to learn more about how to create and officiate a funeral for a child. This is no easy work, and should only be undertaken with a sense of reverence, gentleness and utmost compassion, care and consideration. It's not a task suitable for just anyone. It really isn't. The inner awareness required isn't something you can learn on a quick celebrant-training course. It is acquired through the experience of life, and comes from a place of empathy, emotional articulation, and gentleness. Even if you've already officiated hundreds or even thousands of funerals for adults, what is required for a child's funeral is unlike anything you've experienced before. Personally, I feel that a celebrant who has experienced their own child bereavement will better serve grieving families. It's not essential, but it is helpful.

We have a cultural expectation of life as 'three-score years and ten', and anything less is a life cut short. Alongside this expectation is the idea that a child should outlive the parent, not the other way around. A parent is, by definition, a protector. They're the person for whom the child relies on to keep them safe in this world.

When a child dies, it disrupts the cultural narrative upon which we've built our lives and reminds us of our own fleeting mortality.

Long before I became a celebrant, I walked alongside friends who'd lived through child deaths, and saw for myself the never-ending grief and torment that lived within them. There was no 'get out of jail free' card, nor any expiry date for when their personal hell would be over. Decades later, some of these friends still have nightmares.

My first introduction to child deaths came when I was a child myself. My mother shared stories of her three siblings who had died in infancy during wartime in Germany, and how my Oma's (grandmother) breasts were full with milk to nurture her babies but her arms were empty. My mother, as a young child, was tasked with the job of being breastfeed to help relieve the pressure. "I drank grief" she told me. Her stories have stayed with me year after year. I was gestated in a grieving womb: a place my mother had held babies who didn't come Earthside.

As a mother, I too have known the devastation of holding a baby deep within only to face the bleak and barren landscape that comes with their death. Four times. Four times I've crossed that threshold of grief.

I've often wondered about my Aunty Carole, a generous giver of gifts at Christmas time to her nieces and nephews, and how she'd watch my mother's growing family (eight living children in all) while her own desire to become a mother kept being thwarted with death after death of several babies. Oh how unfair and cruel she must have found it all.

Stolen Spaces

"I did not know what to say to him. I felt awkward and blundering. I did not know how I could reach him, where I could overtake him and go hand in hand with him once more. It is such a secret place, the land of tears."
- *The Little Prince* by Antoine de Saint-Exupéry

Anna was a paramedic and hadn't long been on duty that day when she was called to an accident. No stranger to death, to accidents, to blood, to thinking on her feet, she was skilled at being able to deal with traumatic incidents.

As the driver brought the ambulance to a standstill, she could see people milling around the street. As the first paramedic to arrive, she quickly tried to make sense of the situation before her: a car had hit a cyclist. A child cyclist. A *happy* child out playing on a Summer's day, riding their bike with the sunshine on their skin and all the promises of a carefree childhood. As Anna bent down beside the crumpled body, head smashed and blood on the bitumen, it took several moments before she identified the child: it was her daughter, Alice. Eight years old. Dead.

Once Anna realised it was her beautiful daughter, all her training went out the window. The other paramedics did what they could to pull Anna away, and give her comfort; and to protect her from any further sight of the scene. How does a mother *ever* erase that image? Stop, and read that story again. And then again. Can you understand the horror of it all? Maybe you can imagine. Perhaps you can sense the shock and devastation. Or maybe you'd rather not even have to think about it. You might have even refused to read it a second time. What a luxury.

You, as a celebrant or ceremony writer, can never, will *never*, understand what Anna went through (even if you've been through the death of your child). Unfortunately, there are celebrants who sit with a bereaved parent (family) and say "I know how you feel." One, you *don't* know how they feel. The relationship they had was unique to them and their child. Two, regardless of your background, it is irrelevant to the meeting you have with the family. No way, and in any way, is it about you. Your job, your sacred task, is to *hold the space*. What does that mean?

It means to listen fully, with your whole heart, without judgement, advice, or words of wisdom. You can't fix Anna. You can't fix any bereaved parent.

What *can* you do?

You may lean into their pain, and have the courage to be present. Deep-level presencing is an art and a gift to another which changes our bodily awareness *and* theirs. We can't change the journey Anna is on (or any other person bereaved by a child's death), but we *can* create a space whereby they feel heard and held through our own elevated emotional awareness.

Each human has their own history and with that comes a lifetime of thoughts, ideas, judgements and experiences. When we learn to hold space for others, we do so without bringing judgements with us. We simply are. It is a constant path of growth whereby we, over and over, bring ourselves back to the heart: that place which connects us to the One Heart, and where all humans can unite free of impediments.

How do we know when we are holding space? Our whole being is focused towards the other rather than ourselves. In this space, our ego goes to one side and in its place is grace. As a 'holding container' we don't share relatable stories, nor feel the need to fill the space with questions and chatter.

"You talk when you
cease to be at peace
with your thoughts;
And when you can no longer dwell
in the solitude of your heart
you live in your lips,
and sound is a diversion and a pastime."
– Khalil Gibran

When I was a little girl, I talked so much my mother would send me off to visit the neighbour. She said all my chatter made her ears hurt. Later on, when I learned to write, I expressed myself on the page. Over the years, I've reflected on the above quote by Khalil Gibran, from his book *The Prophet*, and it has fostered a real awareness between speech and silence.

As a funeral celebrant, I've learned to speak even less. This is one of the most important skills we can develop. Speak less. Listen more. Increasingly, I have learned to value silence. It's no longer automatic for me to fill a room or car with music, for example. As much as I love music, I have learned to love silence even more.

Holding space is about deep-level listening so we can be fully present, and yet it is more than this, too. It is about being an emotional container for those in distress, and to be comfortable with 'just being' rather than doing. It is one of the few times in our daily lives where we have to be at home with this.

The questions we ask of a bereaved parent or grandparent or sibling, for example, are based on enquiry. There is a fine line between asking questions to create the ceremony and holding space for another without thinking about the next questions. While they're sharing their thoughts and feelings, we listen. No verbal response is needed. Our facial expressions and body language will show we're listening. This is perhaps one of the hardest skills for most celebrants to develop (whether they do child funerals or not).

Many celebrants (indeed, most people) are not comfortable with silences and seek to 'fill the space'. The more you can become accustomed to it without having to respond or ask another question, the more attuned you'll become to each family you work with. And, increasingly, you'll become aware of how few people can truly hold the space for another. You learn to hear so much of what is unspoken, too. There may be times when it is right to add something, such as "I have no words of comfort but I am here to support you." Or, "Would you like to tell me more about that?" Or, it might be: "I don't know the answer either."

It's not unusual for the bereaved to feel they're being weak and to be worried about admitting that they're struggling. Your job, as the space holder, is to invite deeper connection and to honour their vulnerability.

Don't underestimate how much simply *being present* can provide comfort. Presence doesn't require us to act in a certain way or fill a space with words. This can't be emphasised enough.

One of my favourite quotes is by Cheryl Richardson: "People start to heal the moment they feel heard."

Although most funeral meetings with clients take place just once, it is possible when working with bereaved parents that you'll need more than one meeting. It may be too hard for the parents to talk at the first meeting. This is a time for you to be in each other's company and for them to trust you. It is possible that it can provide a starting point to considering ceremonial ideas. Offer ways for them to think about how to honour their child. It might include writing their child a letter or a few notes about memories.

As they start sharing memories, they will naturally make connections to stories, books, games, music and songs that were important to their child or their memory of the child. They'll reflect on conversations, mannerisms and so on. In turn, this will inspire you with ceremony creation, poem or reading ideas, and ritual narrative and choreography.

Empty Spaces

Halley's son was five hours old when he took his last breath. All the dreams, hopes and wishes Jack and Halley had for their son, Simon, fell to the floor of the hospital room. How was this even possible? There'd been no sign of any problems during pregnancy. The birth had been fairly straightforward. In utter disbelief, Jack and Halley clung to each other.

When you step into the role of being a celebrant for child funerals, this is the energy you'll be be immersed in, and so it is vital you understand your *intention*. With each and every person you work with, before contacting them, breathe in deeply, and go to your heart space. Take some quiet time away from the demands of your life. Ask yourself the following questions. You might like to say them out loud, or write the answers in a journal.

- Why am I doing this?
- What experience will I be offering the family?
- What makes me the right person for them?
- What does this ceremony mean?

♥ A Heart-led Celebrant's Practice ♥

To open your heart, take a few minutes to sit in silence and breathe deeply. Bring your attention to where your physical heart resides in your body. You might become aware of the way it is beating. Go into the quiet and listen to your heart. Say the name of the child whose ceremony you've been asked to officiate. Imagine writing their name across your heart. "I'm here for you. I'm here to share your story. I'm here to remember you on behalf of your loved ones. Show me the way."

Sibling Love

When Marissa left the hospital after the birth of her fifth child, she did so without a baby in arms. Doreen, with a head of thick black hair and long legs, was stillborn. Marissa knew that, when she went into labour, the baby she'd waited for would be dead. It was a long night; thunder growled across the city streets. All that effort, and her reward? Grief. Bone-aching grief.

Hector, Miles, Maggie and Hannah had been so excited to meet their little sister, and while absorbed in grief both Marissa and her husband, Kirk, found ways to comfort their other children.

Encouraging their children to help create Doreen's ceremony gave them a way to express their own feelings of grief, yes, but also love. Miles chose a prayer to read at the funeral, and three-year old Hannah drew a picture of herself on the swing. She wanted Doreen to know how much she was looking forward to being a big sister and playing in the garden with her. Maggie wrote a poem telling Doreen all about the family. Hector helped choose the music, and asked if he could play his accordion, too.

Grief can be utterly debilitating. Everything has changed. There's a compulsion to make the world stop. And yet, it keeps on spinning. Consciously creating a funeral is a way that a family can show their care for a child, and to provide a ceremony which shows what the child means to them.

As a celebrant, part of our role is to help bereaved families, in amongst their confusion, anger, shock and upset, to make choices which will support them not just for the funeral, but in the years to come. If we can do this, then there won't be regrets about how 'the day of goodbye' was created. This last act of love requires care, thought, sacredness, and planning. It also, crucially, offers families a sense of purpose at a time when everything feels so wildly out of control. Don't underestimate the agonising length of time which exists between the death of a child and the funeral. Some families have described it as 'a living hell', 'never-ending', 'unreal', 'longer than a lifetime'.

Soft Space

As is common with any funeral ceremony we officiate, the job is not just about the 20 to 30 minutes we spend at the lectern officiating the service. We are accompanying our chief mourner/s and next of kin from the moment we make first contact right through to the time we part ways with them (whether at the service or later on) during a time of deep upset, confusion, anger, regret, disappointment and hurt. Our ability to be fully present offers a soft space for them to land as they explore some of these emotions.

Grief is one of the greatest wounds we can experience on our human journey. And as with any wound, there is a deep need to apply a balm, a salve, a covering of some sort. As a child, when we scraped our knee red raw there was only one cure: mother love (or the significant caregiver) with the offer of a magic kiss or cuddle. In those moments of harrowing pain, we seek out someone to help make it go away. It is instinctive to search out comfort; pleasure rather than pain. That's universal. As a celebrant, we may not offer magic kisses but a bloody big hug doesn't go amiss (if wanted).

Always ask first! In lieu of these magical mother balms, what we can bring, what we *must* bring, is the soft space of kindness, gentleness and genuine empathy. Empathy is innate. It's not something you can manufacture. You're either an empath or you're not. What you can offer, though, is compassion. It's at the heart of how we show care for humans who are suffering.

Direction

Broadly speaking, a celebrant has two fundamental jobs: to *take* direction from the client and to *offer* direction.

How do we tell the difference? How do we support a mourner towards making choices that will work? How do we say 'no' if something isn't conducive to the ceremony? How do we manage their expectations of ceremony content with the limited time in the crematorium?

Firstly, if the ceremony is in the crematorium, be clear from the outset about the actual ceremony time (not just the slot time) as more often than not funeral directors tend to tell clients the time of the slot (all that means is that is how long from one ceremony to the next). The ceremony time is generally half to one third of the slot time.

Once that is established, and the family understands the restrictions we have to work to, then we can move forward with how to create a beautiful ceremony within that time *and* for it to feel timeless.

Our job walks a tightrope between being employed by the client (subcontracted by the funeral director) and being their guide during ceremony creation, and guardian of the liminal space as they cross the threshold of their child's funeral. At every step of the way we are listening, not just to words but to body language, as we seek to gather what is meaningful to them (and their child). Deep-level listening takes us to a wholly new place, and in my experience it is from this space that we hear our intuition, too, and can loop those inspirations and ideas into a carefully curated creation.

Filling the Space

When it comes to ceremony creation, our job is to guide, support and invite the family to offer ideas and ways which will make the ceremony reflective of the child and be meaningful and honour their beliefs. It is tempting for an inexperienced or busy celebrant to 'fill' the space of a ceremony with readings and music because they feel they have no content. Content is garnered from our deep-level listening. In every memory, there is a story. In every story, a lifetime was lived.

You might think "but the baby died at 12 or 24 weeks in utero. Where's the content?"

The answer is "everywhere!" The content is in:
- Was the pregnancy planned or was it a surprise?
- How did mum's body change in that time?
- When did she first notice baby kick?
- Did she notice other things, like hiccups or moving at certain times of the day?
- What experiences did they have while carrying the baby? Adventures, holidays, outings?

The baby, even at that stage, was an integral part of their lives. Baby went to the movies with them and the farmers' market, and those long strolls on the beach, and pizza night at Harvey's. Baby made its views on sleep-in Sundays strongly known. Ditto garlic bread.

Can you see?

Can you sense how every day is filled with moments and memories? Your job is to bring these 'alive' in your storytelling. And then, from your narrative, it will become clear in which direction you can go with ritual creation. At every step of the way, each intention, each word, each action has to have meaning and bring quality and truth to the ceremony.

If you, as the celebrant, think there's 'no content' you can be sure as heck that your ceremony will feel like that too. If, however, you see how there's a lifetime of stories in every moment then everything changes.

I've made a habit of going through my life and seeing or hearing or smelling something and thinking "There's a novel in that!" And then the ideas flow with full speed. The same principle applies to writing ceremonies. If you open yourself to the possibilities, the material will call out to you in ways you can't even begin to imagine.

♥ A Heart-led Celebrant's Practice ♥
Make this a daily affirmation by either saying it out loud each morning and night or writing it down each morning and night.

"Ideas come to me faster
than I can write,
and they're all brilliant ideas!"

Of course, you can switch the word brilliant to: creative, inspiring, genius, healing - or whatever feels right to you.

Hope

We can't bring other people's children back from the dead. That is the sad and painful and inescapable truth. In countless ways, our hands are tied. Our heart, however, has another way. It has the power of compassionate care and the proffering of hope. Hope is essential to the human spirit. Without it, we wither away. What is hope? It's the expectation that things will be okay.

When a parent has to face the world, without their child, they need to be offered a light, a glimpse of something good in a world that seems so bleak and dark. How do we do this? How do we ensoul our language? In what manner can we bring beauty to the parting of ways they must endure? Is it even possible to offer hope? Is it unrealistic to think we can bring an energy of something that rests on optimism?

Hope gives us a reason to get out of bed in the morning. Hope is a promise that things *will* get better. We can't promise that, of course, but a beautifully crafted and sincerely officiated ceremony can bring solace to the wounded heart. From the knot of grief, our gentleness can help untangle the knot so it's not nearly so tight (something which may take a lifetime to do). Time doesn't heal but in time, and with time, grief softens. It has to. It would be impossible to survive if it stayed the same.

♥ A Heart-led Celebrant's Practice ♥
What does hope mean to you?

How does it show up in your life?

Are there specific words that you associate with hope?

In what way can your writing and your manner instil hope into a child-bereavement ceremony?

Language

Language is something that is constantly evolving, and as funeral professionals our language is changing too. For example, we have moved away from saying "ladies and gentleman" to "friends and family"; to informed consent; away from words like "committed suicide", or "sorry for your loss"; and in time hopefully people will stop saying things like: "they've gone to a better place" or "God must have wanted them" or "at least you've got other children".

What other ways can our language be more mindful? For example, avoiding the tired expression of "I didn't know Jack, but I hear he was a top lad!" *Keep yourself out of it.* You're there to reminisce on behalf of the child's family. Why make it about you and your *lack* of relationship? It speaks of complete disconnection.

Our words have power. The power to hurt. The power to heal. This applies to our spoken words and to our written words.

♥ A Heart-led Celebrant's Practice ♥

Let these words be part of your daily intention setting:

"I am a powerful communicator.
My words heal.
My words bring hope. I write and speak from a place of kindness and clarity."

Silent Spaces

Silence is an art form. Few people allow it to truly permeate their lives. That tendency to switch on the radio, scroll through social media, open a book or magazine, pick up the phone, engage in conversation, is ever present. The majority of domesticated humans fill, fill, fill their *every* waking moment to saturation point. As a Heart-led Celebrant, we recognise that silence offers a respite from the busyness of our work, a retreat from daily life, and an opportunity to create a space in our lives where, free from noise and activity, we can dwell in a place where crystal clarity and intuition become our companions. Have you ever taken a silent retreat? Try 12-24 hours without speaking (or needing to communicate), reading, engaging with social media/emails, and let that experience become a place from which to engage more fully with your true self. The world won't stop just because you take a day off. Your ego, however, will be terrified at the prospect. In a noisy world, the more comfortable you are with silence, the more powerfully you'll be able to hear and read your clients. The quieter you become, the more you can hear.

♥ A Heart-led Celebrant's Practice ♥

Try two hours of mindful silence.
Try four hours.
Six hours.
Build this up to 12 to 24 hours of silence.

Afterwards, reflect on your experience.

Did you make excuses why you couldn't do it?

How has your perspective changed since engaging with silence?

Infant Loss

Termination (medical or personal)

Miscarriage is the spontaneous death of a baby in utero *before* 24 weeks

Stillbirth is the death of the baby *from* 24 weeks gestation

Neonatal is a death occurring *before* four weeks of age

Sudden Infant Death Syndrome is when there is no known cause of death

Accidental is when the death is caused by an accident

Miscarriage

One in four pregnancies ends in miscarriage. The UK has one of the highest stillbirth rates in Europe (according to ONS 4.7 per 1000).

It is important to remember that these statistics are people's *children*.

Being a Child

When does childhood begin? Some would say with the first inhalation. Others differ.

Legal Viability
In England, where I am based, the law currently requires that the body of a child born from 24 weeks gestation be cremated or interred (buried). From a ceremonial point of view, honouring the death of a pre-term child isn't based on 24 weeks and may occur before that date, too.

If you are tasked with creating a ceremony for an infant younger than 24-weeks gestation, you might like to offer a Naming Certificate for the baby. For the purposes of this book, it includes the deaths of all those children who died before birth.

Pre-term Babies

On the day Agnes was preparing to attend her mother's funeral, she received the devastating news that the twins she'd been carrying for five months both had congenital conditions which meant they would not make it full term. A termination would be required to ensure the safety of her own life.

Her sister Layla couldn't understand the grief Agnes was experiencing about the impending terminations. "They're just a bunch of cells! Why are you so upset?" she said in frustration.

Even in an era of increased awareness, there will always be those who lack empathy, kindness and understanding. Unfortunately, sometimes they're the people who are closest to us. For many parents, the love of their child begins with the *dream* of conception, long before sperm and egg connect. For others, it grows with each week of pregnancy.

I was just 19 years old, when I was pregnant with my first child. My boyfriend, in the middle of his university studies as a pathologist, insisted I have an abortion. Science over heart for that man. I chose to keep the baby even though he made it quite clear that I'd be a single parent if I went against his wishes.

Nature, however, had other ideas and my baby died. The journey to hospital was a lonely one. My body was not expelling the baby, but rather holding on. And holding on tightly. My doctor arranged for me to have surgery to remove the body of my dead child. Coming out of anaesthetic, softly sobbing as I said goodbye to my baby, my heart ached at the cruelty of it all.

"What are you crying for? It was dead anyway!" the surgeon snapped at me.

How come he didn't understand? That baby was part of me; created from my very being. My unborn child was a little girl who I expected to have and to hold, to laugh and live with, to run along sandy beaches as we played together or to share a watermelon under sunny skies. In my heart, I'd already dressed my little girl, named her, and made plans for our future. Jessica. Her name was Jessica.

How come he didn't understand?

Little did I know that this would be the first of four pre-term infant deaths.

Thirty years later, and in my work as a funeral celebrant I hear a male celebrant (the one I mentioned earlier) rudely refer to a funeral he'd officiated that day. "Just did a funeral for a foetus," he said with the same uncaring tone as the surgeon from all those years ago. My heart broke all over again. 'Foetus' might be a biological and medical term, but for many parents, it isn't 'just a bunch of cells' forming in the womb.

Why do babies die?

- Problems at birth
- Physical or genetic defects
- Neonatal death
- Accidental death
- Infections in pregnancy
- Placental abruption
- SIDS
- Baby not growing

It is a life. It was a life. It was *their* child. Their child's life.

While I appreciate that each human has a different perspective on when life begins (and different life view), it is important to remember that although many people might consider an unborn baby to be 'disposable', those cells were *fully connected to their carrier*: their mother, and oftentimes the person who helped to create their physical body. Within the space of a mother's womb, millions upon millions of micro-changes happen *every hour*. Of course there is life! Just because it is hidden from our view doesn't make it less of a life.

Unbelievably, there are still crematoria which state they offer funerals for 'non-viable foetuses'. Non-viable might be the medically correct term, but it is not (and never will be) the right language to use for parents who have to cremate or bury their beautiful baby.

There are no words of comfort that you can offer a parent whose baby did not arrive Earthside. There are many things that are said which are, quite frankly unkind (even though that isn't necessarily the intention).

It wasn't their time.
Never mind, you can try for another baby.
Nature knows best.
At least you hadn't met them.
You've got other children.
I know what you're going through. I had a miscarriage too.

Although there's no legal requirement to do so, if your baby died before 24 weeks of gestation, you can still have a funeral.

A Garden Burial
Ebony's tiny body was interred in the family garden. It brought comfort to know she was 'home', and that they could grow flowers), a sign of hope and happiness, over her resting place. A buddleia (butterfly bush) was planted close by, and a patch of wildflower seeds scattered there, too.

A few months later, her parents chose a wooden bench with her name engraved. A few months after that, a small bird bath was added to that part of the garden.

As the seasons come and go, Nancy and Neville reflect on the cycle of life: birth, death, renewal.

In their heartache, they've taken steps to hold their daughter's memory in a way that makes them both smile and cry. A place for comfort and contemplation.

While there's possibly no perfect way to have a funeral for a child, this couple honoured the life and death of their first child in a way that worked for them.

Prayer: *The Light of the Angels Surrounds You*
Poem: *On Angel's Wings*
Song: *Small Bump* – Ed Sheeran
Ritual: *Buddleia Blessing*

"Dearest Ebony, this purple buddleia blossom is a symbol of peace. We will remember you. We are grateful for the joy you brought and the possibilities your presence offered. We love you. Be at peace, sweetheart."

♥ **A Heart-led Celebrant's Practice** ♥
Explore your thoughts and beliefs about funerals for babies who died before term. How do you feel about the legal age of when a funeral is required for a pre-term baby?

The Uncomfortable Silence

What happens when the death of a child is chosen?

When Naomi chose to have a termination, it was one of the most emotionally charged and isolating experiences of her life. With no one to offer her support, pre or post termination, she decided to honour her baby with a private farewell ceremony.

In the time leading up to her baby's ceremony, Naomi gave a lot of thought and care to how she would remember his life.

Darren's remains were placed in a tiny casket for interment in Naomi's garden. The ceremony began with a piece of music: Air on the G String by Bach. After a minute of silence, with her hands shaking and tears streaming down her face, Naomi read out a letter to Darren. In it, she articulated her choice and how she felt it was in his best interests not to grow up in this world. In a heart-felt plea, she hoped that his soul would forgive hers.

As she placed the casket into the open earth, Naomi whispered: "This might be hard to believe but I made this decision from a place of love. You are loved, my baby boy. I wanted you to have a life far better than the one I could ever give you. You will *always* be my son, Darren. You came as a precious gift and now I give you to Mother Earth. Forgive me sweetheart. Forgive me."

The name Darren has Irish origins meaning oak, and a meaningful ritual was created by planting an oak sapling. Naomi placed her letter into the soil, covered it over, then walked away.

Stillborn

I was barely 18 the first time I met someone who'd had a stillborn baby. I was a nanny to her other five other children, and even though it had been seventeen plus years since she'd held her baby in her arms, she still spoke about Claudia every day. Every single day. Claudia was as alive and real in that family as those who were running barefoot on the wooden floors. Years before I became a funeral celebrant, I learned the art of being present. I had no idea back then, as a teenager, just how often stillbirths would show up in my life.

Funeral for a Stillborn Baby
Natasha was quite clear that Cassie Rose wasn't 'born sleeping'. "She's dead, isn't she? If she was asleep, she'd wake up and I'd have my baby!"

The language we use is so important. I, for one, don't use the term 'born sleeping'. While it might bring comfort to some parents, it most certainly doesn't for others. Be client-led at all times.

Cassie's ceremony was a simple eco burial:

Wrapped in a felt shroud, her father carries her to the graveside. A circle of close friends and family surrounds the grave.

Memories: Memories of the hopes and wishes they had for Cassie are shared. The story of Nastasha's pregnancy and Rory's excitement about becoming a dad show the life of Cassie in utero.

Music: *Twinkle Twinkle Little Star* – Mozart (played on a Bose speaker)

Silence: *One Minute of Silence*

Rituals:
100% essential rose-oil drops are added to spring water. A spoon of wildflower honey is mixed into the water. Using the blossom of a red rose, the water is stirred in a circle five times (Cassie was born and died on the 5th day of the 5th month). The blossom is then used to scatter drops of water over Cassie's shroud. This happens five times.

"We use Rose, her namesake; springwater as the source of all life; and honey, to remember her sweetness."

Family and friends scatter fresh pink rose petals over her after interment.

"Darling Cassie Rose, gone from our days but not from our hearts. May you rest beneath this blanket of rose petals knowing you are loved beyond measure."

♥ A Heart-led Celebrant's Practice ♥

You're walking through a graveyard, and see a headstone with the words "Born Asleep". What does this mean to you? Why might it not be helpful to say those words to grieving parents whose baby was stillborn?

Infant

Grace

Grace had lived for just four weeks. A congenital defect meant that her prognosis was not good from the start. Madison and Kevin were determined to make the most of every single day with their daughter, and they did. They wanted Grace to have as good a life as possible and equally, a good death, and a good funeral. Grace's world was rich with love, laughter, long cuddles, lullabies and meeting everyone in her family. Friends came by too, and each person talked to Grace about the place she had in their lives and their hearts. Everyone who met Grace was clear: her life had meaning. And she would be remembered dearly.

Hymn: *Amazing Grace*

Flower Crown: A flower crown from pressed freesias was made. "Freesia symbolises grace under pressure." It was placed on her head inside an open coffin.

Tributes: Each person who met Grace talked about their time with her and what they learned from being in her presence.

Holly & Cinnamon

Holly and her twin sister Cinnamon were born early on Christmas morning just as snow was settling over their town. "Best Christmas present ever!" their father Daniel said as the midwife took a photo of him holding his baby daughters. By January, Cinnamon had passed away from heart failure.

Daniel and Sue knew that they had to honour Christmas as the joyous time they'd always known and loved because they didn't want Holly growing up in the shadow of grief. From the outset, they decided Christmas would be even more special each year.

Ritual: *Holly and Cinnamon's Birthday Pot Pourri*

Items are placed separately on a large table with narrative introducing their symbolism.

- ❖ Cinnamon sticks
- ❖ Dried holly leaves
- ❖ Dried orange slices
- ❖ Dried apple slices
- ❖ Star anise
- ❖ Cardamom pods
- ❖ Whole cloves
- ❖ Clove oil

- ❖ Sweet-orange oil
- ❖ Bay-leaf oil
- ❖ Cinnamon oil

Each mourner is invited to choose an item and either place it into a bowl or sprinkle essential oil onto the dried ingredients. Once combined, they are mixed and then the parents place them into individual bags to be brought out each Christmas.

♥ A Heart-led Celebrant's Practice ♥

A parent's job is to hold their baby, and keep them warm, safe, nourished, loved and protected in this world.

What emotions might parents feel if their baby dies as an infant in arms?

What phrases/statements would NOT be helpful to say to these grieving parents?

Toddler

A Smile Costs Nothing
William was born with an inoperable brain tumour. No one expected him to live so long, but in those two years, four months, three days, and thirteen hours his smile lit up the lives of every single person who met him. His nickname was Smiling William.

Funeral Reading: *A Smile Costs Nothing*

Ritual: *Heart Smile*
"Imagine your heart is smiling. Let that smile spread across your chest. Now let that smile grow wider. And then even wider. Let that smile grow to fill this chapel. When your heart smile reaches to the wall, let it grow some more. Feel it growing bigger and bigger until it stretches right across this city. Can you feel what it is like to be filled with that joy? Each time you do this, you'll have our Smiling William right there with you. A heart smile a day will make this world a far better place."

Invocation: *The One Heart*
"Place your hand on your heart. As you feel it beating gently beneath your hand, know

that we are each connected. Let us give thanks for the ancient heartbeat that connects us to all living beings, to our ancestresses and our ancestors, and to the One Heart. And to Smiling William."

♥ A Heart-led Celebrant's Practice ♥

Take some time in gentle quiet, and place your hand on your heart. As per the above narrative, give thanks to the heartbeat which connects us all.

Around the world, at any given time, parents, siblings and grandparents have just said goodbye to their toddler. Their beautiful child. Sit with this feeling for a while.

What are some ways that toddlers bring joy and enthusiasm to our lives? How might you weave that energy into the ceremony without denying grief?

Young Child

Groceries

It was just an ordinary day when Clarissa was driving to the shops with her two daughters Janella and Anita. The three of them were singing to Taylor Swift's *Romeo and Juliet*. If Clarissa had known that her life would irrevocably change she would never have just popped out for a few groceries that day. Anita died on impact. Janella survived, the spring from the car seat permanently scarring her pretty little face: an ongoing reminder of that fateful day.

Ritual: *Lantern Walk*

Clarissa, John and Janella chose a memorial service following a direct cremation. They assembled a work station in the village hall for mourners to craft willow lanterns. Once all the lanterns were crafted, everyone made their way to a nearby field for a ceremonial walk, and storytelling around a campfire. The lanterns were placed inside the circle of mourners.

The family often sat around their firepit at home, toasting marshmallows, and enjoying stories beneath the starlight. The family's last gift to Anita was a ceremony which reflected something she truly loved.

Out On A Limb

Katy was born to climb trees. When her father, Jeremy, built her a tree house it was like all her Christmases had come at once. Jeremy ensured every aspect of her little hideaway was safe and secure, including the ladder attached to the trunk. But, Katy being Katy, well she was always out on a limb to see how far she could go. A confident climber, it was often Katy who helped rescue the family cat when it couldn't get back down. The whole family was inside the day Katy fell. It would be an hour or so before anyone thought to look for her. She lay, like a crumpled fairy, at the foot of the tree. Later, when her mother was passed some of Katy's belongings, she held her cardigan close to her chest breathing in the scent of her beautiful nine-year-old daughter. As she did so, she felt something in the pocket and reached inside. Typical Katy, there was an assortment of 'treasures': pebbles, a flower, a piece of paper with the words 'make mummy a birthday present', and the wrapper of a lollipop.

Katy's Forever Tree

Although it was because of a tree that their dear Katy died, the family felt it important to honour her love of climbing and natural affinity with trees. Katy's nickname was The Treehugger. No one ever batted an eyelid when Katy said she heard the trees talk to her.

It was decided that the best way to honour her was by planting a tree in her memory. A tree which would grow tall. The family owned their home and garden (so didn't need permission), and chose to have the burial in the far end of the garden and plant the tree there.

Ritual: *Plant a Douglas Fir*

"Sweet, sweet Katy, this tree is planted not only in your memory but so that you have a constant companion, day and night, and a way to climb to the sky. May this silent tree be your friend, your ladder to the stars, and guardian in the silence. This fir tree also symbolises protection. A family seat will be placed here so we can sit and commune with you, although we know that wherever we are, you are too. We'll think of you climbing this tree knowing that you will always be safe, protected and loved."

A spray made from essential oil of pine and spring water is misted over the ceremonial area, and mourners are then invited to share their memories. They have each been holding a pine cone, infused with their stories and memories, and are then invited to place these in a circle around the tree.

♥ A Heart-led Celebrant's Practice ♥

Childhood is part of our journey through life. It's here that we learn about values (our own and other people's) and start making sense of the world.

Reflect on what an 'ideal' childhood might include. For example, a loving and stable home life, walks in nature, freedom, creativity, home baking, family traditions, and so on.

If childhood is part of life's journey and not the destination, how do we make sense of a child's death?

What does it mean to die at this age? Explore your feelings around this.

Teenager

Ross

Ross had been a keen swimmer, and went to the local swimming baths at six o'clock each morning, completing one-hundred laps before school, and each Tuesday and Friday night as part of his swimming club. Davina, his mother, recalled how he was even born in water: the first waterbirth in their family. A promising career awaited him: there was even talk that he had the skills to join the Olympic team.

While other boys his age were on TikTok or hanging out down at the fish-and-chip shop each night having a smoke, Ross was studying performance techniques and learning new ways of improving his style and stroke.

The heatwave caught everyone by surprise, and each person found their own ways to keep cool. That Sunday afternoon Ross was walking his dog, Mitch, alongside the river when two of his mates from school were there swimming beneath the shade of the trees. "Ross, come and swim with us!"

At first, he declined. After all, his mum was expecting him home for dinner in a short while. As he wiped the sweat from his brow, Mitch left his side and entered the water. Despite Ross calling Mitch to 'heel', the dog paddled over to the boys. Frustrated that the dog was not taking any notice, Ross took off his shirt and headed into the river. Nobody knows what happened that day or how he even got into trouble. It was an area of the river that the local lads often swam in, particularly during warmer weather. For a few moments, the school lads thought Ross was just showing off with how long he could stay under water. It took more than a minute for them to realise he was in trouble, but by then it was too late. Far too late.

Ritual: *Wrapping the Towel*
"Ross you came into this world through water, and you left this world in water. Every day you swam your lengths, becoming stronger and more agile, determined to be an elite swimmer.

Today we wrap your swimming towel around you (*the coffin*) as a symbol of keeping you dry between races."
(Mother places towel)

"So that you may always see where you're going, we place your goggles with you too." *(Father places goggles)*

"Ross, you've reached the finish line. We can't go with you, at least not yet. May you now swim at a leisurely pace. Go with the current. Be at peace."

Rebecca and Kimberly
When Ashley and Sue's daughter, Rebecca, confided in them that she was pregnant, they immediately embraced her and offered 100% support. An only child, conceived after ten long years of trying, Rebecca was as deeply loved as any child could be. The news of her pregnancy came when she was just fifteen years old. Although it wasn't the future they'd envisioned for their academically bright child, they were fully accepting and honoured her choice to keep the baby.

As the months rolled by, and the pages of the calendar turned, they were so excited to meet Kimberly. Their granddaughter was due on Christmas day. How glorious the festive season would be! Sue crocheted silk baby booties and helped to decorate the nursery, and Ashley crafted a wooden cradle.

Christmas day came and went, and the days which followed seemed never ending even though they knew only a few percent of babies are born on their due date. Kimberly was born just shy of midnight on the 31st of December. The labour was hard, and unseen complications and medical error took their toll on mother and child. Rebecca died before meeting her baby, and Kimberly passed away within minutes of birth.

Ashley and Sue stayed in the room with them and spent the first day of the new year paralysed with shock. There were so many questions which needed answering, medically, but the biggest question of all was: "Why our daughter and granddaughter?"

Mother and daughter were buried in the same grave, with Kimberly tucked into her mother's arms. "It's her rightful place," Sue said.

Ritual: *Pine Brushing*
"With the brushing of this coffin with pine, a symbol of longevity, we tell you softly today: our love for you both will remain evergreen."
(brush the coffin with a branch of pine)
The ceremony, at a natural burial ground, also honoured the meaning of their names:

Rebecca, meaning *to tie or bind*; Kimberly, *royal fortress meadow*.

Ritual: *Meadow Flowers & Pretty Ribbons*
Small hessian bags containing the seeds of meadow flowers were set on a butler's table. Each mourner was invited to take one, and then tie a pink ribbon into a bow around the top of the bag. Arrangements had been made to have the grave filled in after interment while the mourners were still there. After the grave was covered, the bags were placed on the soil and then lightly covered with more soil. Ashley and Sue walked around with an ornate watering can and ensured they were well watered. Two small paper crowns, with the names Kimberly and Rebecca, were placed at the head of the grave.

Savannah
It's fair to say Savannah grew up on the back of a horse. The livery stables were as important to her as the air she breathed. Many people called her a horse whisperer for she had the most amazing way with horses, even those considered too difficult for their owners to handle. What happened to her wasn't something anyone could have foreseen. Henry was the most laid-back pony she'd

ever known. There wasn't an inch of his body that she couldn't touch or brush. So the day he kicked her in the head, it was a complete mystery. Only the coroner's report would reveal the truth: Henry had been bitten on his hind leg by a hornet, and the sting caused him to lash out. It was just a matter of Savannah being in the wrong place at the wrong time: she had been leaning over, cleaning a watering trough. Death was instant.

Her parents said it gave them 'some' comfort to know she didn't suffer. Of all the horses Savannah had known and loved, Henry was always her favourite: she'd helped raise him from when he was a foal. His mother, a roan-coloured mare named Apple, had died during his delivery. Savannah always felt like she was Henry's adoptive mum.

Ritual: *Golden Horseshoe*
A horseshoe is spraypainted gold and thin colourful ribbons are threaded through the holes.

A different coloured ribbon is used to represent each year of her life. As it is threaded, a highlight from that year is shared. It is then placed on the coffin after the words of committal.

"Savannah, this first ribbon is for the day you were born. Bum first, your mum said, and an emergency caesarean which brought you into this world. Right from the start you liked to do things differently."

"This fourth ribbon is for when you could ride on your own without an adult. Your parents remember the day you insisted that you didn't need anyone to lead you."

Joseph

Joseph had dabbled in drugs since the first day of secondary school when an older boy dared him. From then on, it was always just a bit of fun and a way to bond with those in his social circle. By the time he was studying for his A levels, he'd become addicted. It wasn't his intention to overdose. All he wanted to do was settle his anxiety. When his mother found him, he'd fallen asleep in his own vomit. No matter how much she tried, she couldn't get the image out of her head.

Reflecting on the anxiety which had always plagued him, a ritual was chosen to symbolise calm.

Ritual: *Calming Chamomile*

"Joseph, as we lay you to rest, we do so with reverence and the hope that you are now at peace. Chamomile for calm. Lavender to cleanse the unrest. Valerian for deep sleep. Lemon balm to soothe the nerves. St. John's Wort to relieve anxiety. You are loved beyond measure."

(*The ritual grinding in a mortar and pestle, and then scattering, of dried herbs, chamomile, lavender, valerian, lemon balm and St. John's Wort, over the coffin, is followed by one minute of silence.*)

Toby

Toby and Trina were the best of friends even though, personality-wise, they were like chalk and cheese. They were also twins. Toby's death, by suicide, after he walked in front of a train, left the family and community in a deep state of shock, but no one more so than his sister, Trina. Toby had always been the upbeat of the two, while Trina was reserved and tended to have mood dips. No one, especially Trina, understood what happened. There'd been no sign of depression. Alee and Martin, their parents, distraught at their son's death, also had to face the reality that Trina was now on suicide watch.

"Toby, you brought so much laughter to people's lives that it seems inconceivable we're here today. We remember you as a bright young man with the whole world ahead of you. Your plans to study accountancy were just a breath away. Our grief at your passing doesn't add up."

Ritual: *Abacus*
This abacus was one of Toby's childhood toys. An abacus is a counting frame, and these have been used since ancient times. It is a symbol of abundance. Today, we give thanks for the riches Toby brought to our life through his laughter, enthusiasm and athleticism. We use it today to add up the years of his life: Fifteen years of love, laughter, family, friendship and study. Fifteen years where he gave his best self to others. Fifteen years of understanding the way things fit together. In a moment, Alee and Martin will move the discs on the abacus, one at a time, as we share how he lived each of those years."

As ever, the language we use is important. We don't condemn someone because of the manner in which they died. When a person chooses to end their life, we say they died of suicide or by suicide.

We don't say 'committed' for any other type of death so there's no reason or need to say it for suicide. When my father died, he didn't 'commit a car accident'. We don't say 'Susan committed heart failure' or 'Jeremy committed dementia'.

If you work as a funeral celebrant, you must bring the same compassion and care of language to the awareness of death by suicide as you would for any other death.

Be client-led regarding if they want mental-health awareness raised in the opening address of the ceremony. At all times, recognise that suicide is chosen in response to heartbreak, struggle, pain or addiction. They weren't seeking attention or being selfish.

Ritual: *Pockets in my Shroud*
Angelia had four months to plan her funeral. As a naturally creative person, when faced with her mortality, she leaned into the creativity even more. Throughout her life, friendships had always been easy for her, and her days were filled with loving people. She'd decided though, that her funeral would be invitation only as she didn't want her parents

overwhelmed (or "feeding the 5,000", as she called them). Despite that, she had a request. While living out much of her remaining time at the hospice, she had her mother bring in a small sewing machine, sewing box, and some of her favourite clothes. Angelia's aunty Maggie often used to say "aint no pockets in a shroud". It always seemed like a funny saying, and so when contemplating her funeral, Angelia decided that she wouldn't have a coffin. She'd have a shroud. A shroud with pockets! Each day, when she had some energy, Angelia would sit at the sewing machine and stitch. Unravelling some of her favourite clothes, she then removed pockets. Day by day she sewed them all together until she had a complete shroud made from pockets.

Satisfied that she'd be held, within her own familiar clothes, there was one more request: for those invited to the funeral to write a note or letter, and to place it into a pocket for Angelia to take with her. At the ceremony, they were asked to stand around her, holding hands.

Ritual: *A Pocketful of Love*
"Angelia, each pocket here is a symbol of abundance: the wealth of all your talents, joys, and secrets, too. Each of your friends has written

you a love letter, and in a moment they'll place it inside a pocket for you. Take this love, no matter where you're flying amongst the stars, and know that this life of yours was valued by everyone who knew you. Your parents will start by each placing a rose-quartz love heart with their letter into a pocket. Angelia, you chose a pocket for each of your parents: the turquoise embroidered silk one for your Mam, and the forest-green corduroy for your Dad."
(place the quartz, and then invite other mourners to place their love letters)

Words of Committal
"Angelia, the time has come for us to part ways. It is with tenderness, love and care that we offer your mortal body to rest here in the eternal embrace of Mother Earth. May you, your essence, return to The Starmaker."

***

Teenagers live in that liminal space between childhood and adulthood. They're freedom-lovers, for the most part, and are seeking to establish their identity and place in this world. As they move towards independence, it means leaving behind the ways of their early years. At this stage of life we're getting a stronger sense of who the person will be when they go out into the world as an adult. There are dreams just within reach. Initiations yet to experience. In some ways, being a teenager is like being a rocket about to launch into space. We have a sense of the trajectory. There is power in takeoff.

And then the mission is aborted. There will be no adulthood. The story of their life is over.

♥ A Heart-led Celebrant's Practice ♥

Hold each of these teenage stories with you. Sit in their worlds for a while. Tonight you'll be having dinner, maybe watching a TV show or taking part in a hobby. Your life continues as per your expectations. You might be living your dream life or just making do but whatever path you're on, you're still here. You're living your life. These teenagers are not. And their families have to get up each morning with a life-sized hole in their hearts.

Explore your own teenage years. What memories do you have? Reflect on that feeling of not being a child and not being an adult. Immerse yourself in that part of your life once again.

To write about the life of a teenager, it can help to remember that threshold in our own life. Regardless of how different each teen's life story is, there are universal themes of maturing emotionally, physically and psychologically. And within those rapidly changing areas, there remains a need for: boundaries, role models, ways to alleviate tension, and opportunities to build self-esteem.

In your role as a celebrant, there is a rich world of possibilities to explore when creating a panoramic view of a teenager's life. This linguistic landscape that you carefully craft with your wordsmithery is a legacy you leave with the family and friends in mourning.

Young Adult

There are times, certainly for our purposes as a celebrant or vicar or minister, when a young adult (that is, someone over the age of 18) may be classed as a child for our ceremonial planning. For example, in my experience, someone who has spent their childhood in a hospice may remain in the children's hospice after their 18th birthday and continue to stay there for several years.

Damon was 24 when he passed away. For ten years, he'd lived mostly in the children's hospice. Prior to his diagnosis, he'd lived a full and happy childhood. No one had an inkling of the syndrome which would soon show up and debilitate him completely. Due to staying in the children's hospice, he retained a childlike quality never experiencing the milestones common to young adults: like graduating from school or university, hanging out with mates, first dates, sex, road trips, driving a car, and starting a new job.

Damon helped to plan his funeral and was clear that he didn't want a sombre or sad occasion. He wanted a funfair! The ceremony, he decided, would be held in a bouncy castle! There'd be candy floss, clowns on stilts, and hot dogs.

Although his request to be attached to a rocket and sent to the Moon couldn't be fulfilled, there were fireworks. As they lit up the sky that night, the hearse drove silently away ready for his direct cremation the following morning.

Sven

Sven was loving his new life fresh out of secondary school. Not only was he about to start a new job, he was also dating. In his own words, "Life's perfect, Mam!" The first car he bought was an old second-hand sports car; something he was able to purchase from saved inheritance and Summer job earnings. That day, the day he died, he wasn't even driving it fast. Death was instant: decapitated when a haulage truck ploughed into him. I remember his mother's words as reflected in a poem she wrote and how the trio was now a duo, and "the tune is so different".

Happy Helen

Saskia told me about how her sister Helen was driving back home for the weekend when a car hit her head on. It was important to Saskia to share with me all the hopes and dreams her sister had: she was engaged to Phil, and they were planning to start a family. When a life has been cut 'short', the sharing of hopes and dreams is important. Obviously it highlights the 'cutting short'; however, it also shows them living a life of vitality. And that, must surely give others hope? For what is a life without dreams?

♥ A Heart-led Celebrant's Practice ♥

How might a young adult, say someone in their early to mid-twenties, be considered a 'child' in ceremony planning?

Write down three key points that would need to be taken into consideration.

Always Someone's Child

No matter how we age, we're always someone's child. I've lost count of how many funerals I've officiated for adults whose parents had to say goodbye. That grief isn't any less traumatic if their child was twenty, forty, fifty or seventy than if they were five. You may think "Yes it is! Their child lived a full life." Yes, they may have had a full life from the 'three-score years and ten' perspective, but from the parents' view it is their *child*.

Tom and Margaret were in their eighties when Dina passed away following a stroke. She was 65, and their eldest daughter. People foolishly said things like "At least your other children are still alive." How is that helpful? In what way is that compassionate?

Dina was a mother, grandmother, wife, sister, aunty and 'bloody good friend'.

No matter the age or stage, your child's death changes you. As a celebrant, we must never forget that.

Sudden Deaths
& Slow Deaths

Does it make a difference the manner in which a child dies? Yes, to some degree. With sudden deaths, the shock adds a whole new level to grief. In some cases, there is guilt, too. One of the hardest parts is not having had a chance to say goodbye or rectify any difficulties or misunderstandings in the relationship.

When a person has had a long, slow and drawn-out death, while it does offer the chance to say goodbye and bring a sense of closure before the death takes place, it can bring its own layers of guilt: primarily around any feelings of relief that the unbearable situation is now over. And yet, even when there may have been *years* of slowly letting go, when the last breath has passed, there is nothing which can prepare one for the feeling of finality.

As a celebrant, we need to carry within us a deep awareness of the many layers of grief.

♥ A Heart-led Celebrant's Practice ♥

Explore your thoughts and feelings about sudden deaths and slow deaths, and the impact this might have on a grieving family.

How might your role differ, in terms of family meetings, writing the script and officiating the ceremony, depending on the type of death the child experienced?

Space & Place

One of the first decisions a family must make when planning their child's funeral is where to hold the ceremony. In many cases, this decision will be made before your entry into their life as a celebrant. However, if you are in a position to offer suggestions or are asked for advice, you can let a family know that their options can go beyond the two often-chosen ones of crematorium chapel or cemetery. A ceremonial space does not have to be where the burial or cremation takes place.

- Crematorium chapel
- Graveyard or Cemetery (a graveyard is part of a church; a cemetery is not connected to a church)
- Funeral Parlour
- Church or non-denominational chapel
- Home
- Garden
- Natural burial site
- Beach
- Woodland
- Orchard
- Meadow

Examples of other venues which have been chosen (with permission):

- favourite café
- library
- museum
- bookstore
- archery club
- swimming club
- forest school
- local small aerodrome
- farmyard
- BMX track
- field

♥ **A Heart-led Celebrant's Practice**♥

Consider your local community, and write down five possible places where a funeral or memorial service could be held.

What would be the advantages and disadvantages of each of these places?

The Final Journey

Although, in our culture, we are used to seeing a hearse carry the coffin or shroud there is no legal requirement for one to do so. If the family wishes to transport their child to the ceremonial site and place of cremation or interment, then that is their right. In the UK, the only legal requirement is that the body is covered when being transported in public. It doesn't have to be a coffin.

Here are some examples of other options:
- Limousine
- Horse and cart
- Unicorn horse
- Specialist vehicles
- Bike
- Pillion bike
- Go-kart
- Bier (hand-pulled cart)

Upon arrival at the ceremony venue, a baby or young child can be carried in arms, pushed in a pram, or placed on a pull-along wagon.

♥ A Heart-led Celebrant's Practice ♥

Reflect on the following words written by Sara Rian:

> we are carried.
> in bellies. in arms.
> in love. in hope.
> in caskets. in urns.
> in grief. in memories.
> our whole lives
> and into the next
> we are carried.

Set a timer, and for five minutes write on the theme of being 'carried' in relation to childhood and child death.

Ceremonial Work

Bringing the ceremony together

- Meeting/s with the family
- Creativity, inspiration & intuition
- Writing draft
- Creating rituals
- Writing prayers or blessings
- Rehearsal of the ceremony
- Officiating the ceremony
- The gentle goodbye

Interview or Invitation?
There are, broadly speaking, three types of interviewing styles:
- Structured
- Semi-structured
- Unstructured

Interview v Invitation? For many people, an interview equals stress. Interviews can make people feel like they're on trial or being interrogated or like they're sitting an exam.

Invitational-style information gathering is based on conversation; it's friendly and leads to more truthful answers and allows you to ask unexpected questions. A great conversation is inspiring. Your goal as a celebrant is to learn more; to gather information.

Recently, I was with a trio of sisters, in their seventies, and we were having a conversation about their mother who'd just passed away. One of them confided that their memories of mother weren't positive. "She was always crying," said one. "Never did the housework," said another. "We came home from school and there was never a cooked meal." "Maybe she was depressed," chimed the other as if the thought had never occurred to them before.

"Did your mother ever lose a baby or child? Has there been a death?" I asked gently. Their mother sounded to me as if she had experienced severe and ongoing post-natal depression as well as grief. "Yes," they said. "Our baby brother."

Another sister said "That wouldn't have bothered her though!"

"How did he die?" I asked. Their baby brother had died through a forceps injury during birth (medical mismanagement).

I share this example because when we go into a meeting with our clients and arrive with a set list of questions we risk missing out on truth. My own working style as a celebrant is completely unstructured conversation.

♥ A Heart-led Celebrant's Practice ♥

Consider the ways in which approaching a family meeting with a list of set questions might inhibit honest conversation. For example:

Where was John born? What school did he go to? What were his favourite hobbies? Did he have any good friends?

Compare it to questions which might arise in an organic conversation, with ample time to answer and explore each question.

Is that John's BMX bike out on the driveway? Where did he ride? How many kids are in that club? When did he first become interested in BMX riding? It's an exciting form of sport. Did that excitement show up in his life in other ways?

Saying Goodbye

The purpose of a funeral is to say goodbye as we let go of the mortal physical body of someone's beloved.

A celebrant-led ceremony is co-created with the family through gentle and compassionate conversation, and although we might create, design and write the ceremony and its rituals, it should be done in careful consultation with those involved. My experience as a funeral celebrant is based on *always* sharing the full script (not just the eulogy) well ahead of the ceremony date so that my chief mourner/s have time and space to be sure the ceremony will meet their needs.

Regardless of the age of the child, the ceremony creates a space, privately or publicly, to:
- say their name
- remember the stories about them
- to share grief
- to say farewell

For those funerals where it is for a baby who hadn't yet been named, ask if they'd like a naming or dedication ritual, too.

♥ A Heart-led Celebrant's Practice ♥

Why is it important to remember and share the stories of a child's life at their funeral?

How might the collective sharing of grief be helpful for the bereaved family?

Saying Their Name

♥ A Heart-led Celebrant's Practice ♥

Say your name out loud. Just your first name is fine. Say it again. And once more. This is a word you're so familiar with. Throughout your life you've heard it, seen it, felt it. Over and over again. It's part of you. Now write your name down five times.

1.
2.
3.
4.
5.

How does this feel?

What do you experience when you hear or see your name?

Throughout our life, our name is spoken in countless ways. It may be shouted at you or sung to you. Maybe it was whispered and used to woo you; perhaps it has been cried through tears or possibly while laughing. Has it been uttered in disappointment or deliberated on during distress?

Who calls your name? Family, friends, strangers? For some of us, our name will be called thousands of times in the course of our lifetime. For some, very few times. And what of those who weren't even named? May we remember them, too.

Names hold the energy of a person. It is so much more than a label or an identifier. It's also an invocation. When a child dies, there is the fear that their name will disappear on the breeze; ghostlike in the distance.

As with any funeral ceremony, we say the name throughout our service. This becomes more so for a child whose name won't be called millions of times.

When working with a family, think about how that name feels. How it sounds. Where do you wear it in your body? Let the name really sit with you. Before you prepare to write the ceremony, try saying the name in many different ways. Feel the name. Touch the name. Taste the name.

This is the name the child's parents had consciously chosen and had expected to say for many, many years. Really let that sit with you.

Allow yourself to fall in love with the name as if it was one you'd chosen yourself. This level of connection that you, as the celebrant, create with this child's name will shine through authentically in the service.

During the ceremony you'll not only be talking about that person, you'll be speaking directly to them for the committal or sharing tributes, and for any prayer or blessing you write. Don't let them be a stranger to you.

Every name carries a vibration. When you tune into the vibrational energy and frequency of the child's name you'll be able to match that in your ceremonial writing: *your* gift to that child.

Writing Their Name

Writing the child's name is also a powerful way of honouring their essence. My preference in symbolic work is to do something three times. So, in this case, I'd write the name three times or ask the assigned person (e.g. a parent) to do so.

Here are some ways to write the name:
- With a feather in the air
- Using flowers on long stems, such as sunflower or gerbera, either in the air or placed on the ground or on paper
- Flower heads, such as daisies and dandelions
- Pebbles
- Rope
- Marbles
- Bark
- Moss
- Rosehips
- Pinecones
- Dinosaurs
- Barbie Dolls
- Coloured Ribbons
- Matchbox cars
- Conkers

- Acorns
- Stuffed teddy bears
- Pen or pencil
- Charcoal
- Chalk
- Paint
- Macrame

♥ A Heart-led Celebrant's Practice ♥
Make a list of all the different ways you could write a name.

Writing A Blessing

The parents may have chosen, and wish to be guided to find, a reading to include. There are many beautiful readings suitable for a child's funeral. They might also request a prayer or a blessing. A blessing is an offering. It comes from a place of grace, care, respect and reverence.

Let us not measure your life
by the number of breaths taken;
Let us take comfort that we love you
and you live on in our hearts;
May you and I and they
go forward from this day
Enriched by the privilege
of having known you.
May we cherish the moments
Which brought us together
And the love which will linger
in the circle of our lives.

♥ A Heart-led Celebrant's Practice ♥

Write two examples of a blessing you could include in a child-bereavement ceremony. Perhaps write one for those of a religious or spiritual faith and one for those who are humanist.

When Words
Aren't Enough

There are times, no matter how gentle, thoughtful and inspired our words are, when the ceremony narrative may not be enough. This is when silence or quiet prayer and contemplation, music (instrumental) and rituals enhance the ceremony.

As in life, we don't have to fill every space with 'noise'. Allow 'white space' into your ceremonies. It can be through dedicated silence or it can be in the mindful way you pause between sentences or ensuring that you speak throughout the ceremony in a much slower, more deliberate and softer way than you do in everyday conversation.

One of my favourite quotes is:

> *"When words are inadequate,*
> *have a ritual."*
> \- Anon

♥ A Heart-led Celebrant's Practice ♥

How might consciously bringing more silence into your life, and specifically your celebrant practice, offer a cushion to those who are grieving?

Love Letters

Reading love letters and tributes is, I find, so much harder than sharing something I've written. There is an absolute art to speaking on someone's behalf at such a personal and intimate moment. As with the rest of the ceremony, be 100% fluent with your script. Rehearse, rehearse, rehearse, so that you are making maximum eye contact and engaging with people, rather than having your head down. If the tribute is addressed directly to the child, look at the coffin or shroud.

Take your time.

Breathe slowly.

Allow the full depth of feeling behind the words to shine through.

For Lucia
You were my everything: the air that I breathed, the reason for being. I can't believe that we're living this day, and you're not; and that I can't hold you anymore.

I'll never hear you run into the kitchen telling

me about what you did at school or showing me your latest drawing, or the way you'd make me laugh whenever you dressed Muffles, our cat. I'll never again hear you tell me about your hatred of mushrooms, love of olive bread, and that you're going to marry Mary Poppins when you grow up.

Lucia, light of my life, I will love you as long as the stars keep shining. Mam. Xxx

***

Frank, you were my mate. My best friend. I was the proudest grandfather in the world the day you were born. Every time you came for a sleepover, your Glammy and I would be so excited. You're sleeping now, but we can't be with you. You'll always be in our hearts. I'll always remember you sitting on my lap for storytime. You'll always be my little mate. Love, Pops.

♥ A Heart-led Celebrant's Practice ♥

What inner gifts will allow you to share a bereaved person's tribute as if they were speaking the words out loud themselves?

Closure

The moment of closure is a defining space in any funeral. Quite often it is seen as the long-lasting seconds during which the curtain closes or the coffin/shroud is interred. There are many other ways, too, which can include a parent or be done on behalf of parents/family that are personal and meaningful.

In my funeral-celebrant practice, I leave the lectern at or for the committal (depending on the audience size/if it is being livestreamed and if there's a risk of not being heard) and say the words while touching the coffin. I always bow before leaving the coffin.

Various funerary-closure rituals include blessing the coffin. This can be done by sprinkling sacred water (with a bunch of lavender, for example), or touching the coffin three times with a white feather or flower of choice, or perhaps covering the coffin with their favourite blanket or family heirloom quilt. It might be placing their favourite food on the coffin/shroud, such as chocolate. Graveside, it could be scattering feathers, flowers, leaves on the coffin just before or after interment.

Bunches of lavender (for deep and eternal rest), buddleia for peace after struggle, rosemary for remembrance, for example.

♥ A Heart-led Celebrant's Practice ♥
Why is closure important when a parent (or other loved one) is at a funeral for their child?

The Scar

Some of the best funeral celebrants I know are those who have experienced the death of a child. Again, they don't know how their client feels but they do know what *their* experience was like, and this allows them to navigate the two-fold path of when to stand back and when to lean in.

It's never our job as a funeral celebrant to tell a client about our back story. But of this, you can be sure: *every moment of your own life informs your work, and you take this with you to every family visit and every funeral you officiate.* And it is for this reason I always recommend that you sit with your own bereavement for some time before entering this work.

Work from the scar,
not the wound.

It is said that "We can't heal what we can't feel," and also that we "Teach best what we need to learn." Our journey as a funeral celebrant is a constant learning and unravelling. Our most important work is our inner work; the work invisible to others but highly visible by the presence we offer.

♥ A Heart-led Celebrant's Practice ♥
Write down your wounds regarding child deaths (whether your own or someone you know personally).

Have these wounds begun healing as scars? If so, explore your scars around these deaths.

Children Grieve

I've never met an adult yet who, denied a funeral in childhood for a loved one, has a sense of closure around that death. While the choice to keep children away from funerals is done with the best of intentions, it doesn't necessarily have the desired effect of protecting them.

Every funeral I create, when I know there will be children in attendance, is certain to leave them with *affirmation* of the life we've honoured, and a sense of beauty about how we say goodbye.

Where possible, actively involve them (at age-appropriate levels). I find that children often come up with the most wonderful ideas or quotes that weave so beautifully into ceremonies. It's a joy to see their little faces light up when their input is included. They're learning from us all the time and yet there's so much we can learn from them, too, if only we take a moment to stop and listen.

Children grieve too, and with care, respect, guidance and understanding, can be part of the collective expression of farewell in ways that are healing, helpful and beautiful.

♥ A Heart-led Celebrant's Practice ♥
How do you think children grieve?

Is child grief different to adult grief?

What are your thoughts about children attending funerals?

Is there an age in which they should be kept away?

What might be some of the ways you can include children in ceremony creation?

Your First Funeral

Nothing will prepare you for the moment you walk into the bereavement room in a hospice and are asked by the family to meet their dead child.

Nothing will give you the confidence to meet with a newly bereaved family and see the baby's clothes laid out on a chair next to an empty crib.

Nothing will prepare you for that moment a tiny coffin or shroud is carried down the aisle of a chapel by a wailing parent.

Nothing in your celebrant-training course gives you the psychological and emotional strength and equilibrium necessary when immersed in an ocean of grief: everyone in the chapel sobbing without restraint.

Nothing you do can set you up, emotionally, for when the coffin is interred down into the earth, and the family are crumbling alongside. Nothing.

Nothing you can do or say will bring comfort to a family when they walk away from the graveside and back into their life. Without their child.

All of these things are
initiatory experiences
and must be met
with the reverence they deserve.

Whatever discomfort and angst we feel pales into insignificance compared to what the parents/family are going through. It doesn't make our feelings irrelevant, just different.

When you have an imminent child funeral, it is important to schedule space in your diary and limit the number of other funerals you take on. This work is different, and you're on a fast track to burnout if you think it doesn't need space either side of the ceremony.

♥ A Heart-led Celebrant's Practice ♥

Consider the spaces in your life. Do you have the emotional and psychological room (space) to hold a grieving family who has to say goodbye to their child?

Identify these spaces.

What makes you think you have this capacity?

Giving Yourself Space

You won't ever forget the role you played in a family's child-bereavement story. This will affect you like no other funeral experience. It is important to have self-care practices in place whether as permanent fixtures in your life or specifically for these times.

Number one is to have a mentor. This may be another professional celebrant experienced in child funerals or a counsellor or caring funeral director.

- Don't take on too many child funerals (paid or unpaid).
- Don't isolate yourself from friends and family. Share your feelings with them. Sometimes celebrants will try to protect their loved ones but it's at a cost to themselves. You need someone to hold space for you.
- Exercise: walk, run, swim, cycle, dance, yoga, etc. Move your body and keep the energy flowing. Grief accelerates adrenaline. Movement is far better for you than sitting down with a cup of tea.
- Engage in crafts or leisure interests which

nourish you such as gardening, baking, cooking, dancing, knitting, listening to music, hula hooping.

- Developing a reflective-writing practice is also beneficial.
- Do what you need to do to keep yourself functioning well even if it means going to bed with a hotwater bottle and having a cry. There's no shame in this. Do whatever it is that helps you recover.

♥ A Heart-led Celebrant's Practice ♥

Write a list of twenty self-care practices to support you in your child-bereavement work.

Vicarious Trauma

One thing a child-bereavement celebrant needs to be aware of is vicarious trauma, also known as secondary trauma. This happens when you've been exposed, as an indirect experience, to someone's traumatic event.

When we hear a person's story and all the details of their trauma, it can easily lodge into our being. I remember feeling this strongly, physically and emotionally, when I heard Anna's story (page 12) for the first time. She was physically touching me as she recounted the day she found her daughter lying dead on the road. I could feel her shock and upset seeping into every cell of my being.

When we work closely with the bereaved, it's an essential part of our job to listen closely and be emotionally and mentally present to their experiences. Now, that might go without saying, and that it's par for the course to prepare ourselves for this; however, we don't have, readily available in this industry, the support systems in place to help us through these times.

I doubt very few celebrants would have learned about secondary trauma in their celebrant-training studies.

When our clients recollect their traumatic stories, it can invade our own psyche. It's important to recognise that although the trauma happened to someone else, the impact on you, as the celebrant, isn't to be dismissed as insignificant.

While it's natural for any empathic person to react to someone else's traumatic stories, for some celebrants the impact might have long-term consequences. One of the reasons vicarious trauma is less understood than other forms of PTSD, is that being exposed to someone who is suffering from trauma is often seen as less dramatic.

How might you recognise signs of vicarious trauma?
- Depression
- Anxiety
- Sleep problems
- Poor sense of self
- Emotionally depleted
- Sense of hopelessness
- Difficulty eating

If you feel yourself starting to change after your exposure to families who are experiencing deep-level trauma, look out for the following and seek help:

• When you're unable to let go of your feelings of sadness or anger about the client's situation

• Feeling existential guilt that they're the ones who are suffering and not you

• When your thoughts about your client dominate your day and night, and stop you thinking about other things

• Having inclinations (fantasies) of rescuing them

• Becoming increasingly negative and feeling hopeless

• Feeling disconnected from other clients, and emotionally numbing yourself

• Going way beyond your professional remit to help (at the cost of your own wellbeing)

Recognise vicarious trauma, and:

• Practise self-care

• Nurture yourself physically and mentally

• Ensure you engage in pleasure and interests not connected to work

• Remember you're not responsible for your client's wellbeing. Give them support,

and show them support options. Stay focused on your role.
•   Seek support from professionals and from experienced celebrants to debrief

Child Funeral Charity

The **Child Funeral Charity** (CFC) is there to assist families in Wales and England who need financial help for the funeral of a baby or child. CFC can help with baby and child funerals in England and Wales from 12 weeks gestation to 16 years of age.

While some funeral directors and celebrants don't charge fees, there are other expenses that still need to be paid.

CFC can assist by either paying funeral directors for certain items or by using the suppliers who work with them to obtain items such as flowers, orders of service and plaques.

As a celebrant, you can make referrals for financial support if you have knowledge of the bereaved family's circumstances.

childfuneralcharity.org.uk

Child Funeral Fund

In addition to CFC, there is also the government's **Child Funeral Fund**.

Fees for cremation and burial can be met, for the most part, by this government funding. To be eligible, the child must be under 18 at the time of death, and the burial or cremation must take place in England. This is not income tested. gov.uk/child-funeral-costs

If a family is on any benefits, they also have access to: gov.uk/funeral-payments

Do We Charge?

There are two distinct answers to the question: Do we charge a fee for officiating funerals for children?

There are many celebrants who will categorically state that it is wrong to charge for funerals for those under the age of 18. What about someone who dies aged 18 and one hour or day, or 18 and one week? Is the parent of that person grieving less because their child is now officially an adult?

And there are those celebrants who charge either their normal fee, or part thereof, because they recognise the unique qualities and skillset involved.

This role requires the gifts of empathy, awareness, intuition, creativity and more. It is a *highly specialised* job. Does that mean we offer these as a charity? That is completely your choice. Be clear, though, that whatever choice you make it has to be right for you. At no level should another celebrant or funeral director make you feel guilty if you choose to charge. There is NO right or wrong answer to this. It is up to the individual. In no other workplace would we ask someone to give 10 to 15 hours of time for free.

A doctor working alongside a dying child or a coroner won't be working for free. Why would we expect a celebrant to do so? Why have we made money ugly? I've heard the argument used that a parent doesn't choose for their child to die. I don't imagine an 80-year-old woman chooses for her husband to die either.

There's also the risk of becoming known for officiating child-bereavement ceremonies, and ending up with doing a lot of work for free, and as a result having to turn away paid work. These are things you must consider.

♥ A Heart-led Celebrant's Practice ♥

Is there really a cut-off age to adulthood?

Consider how you feel about charging for a funeral when person who died was one day or one week into legal adulthood.

List five strong reasons *not* to charge for meeting with a family, and creating, writing and officiating a beautiful child-bereavement ceremony.

1.
2.
3.
4.
5.

List five strong reasons *to* charge for meeting with a family, then creating, writing and officiating a beautiful child-bereavement ceremony.

1.
2.
3.
4.
5.

Crafting
Beautiful Ceremonies

To craft a beautiful ceremony begins with deep-level listening. When holding the space for a grieving family, we can become open to ideas, inspiration and intuitive impulses which draw us to the right feel and tone, language and symbolism. There is no one right way to create a funeral for a child. And there's certainly no template. For me, listening goes beyond what I hear with my two ears. It's a type of clairaudience (extrasensory listening); a listening that goes *beyond* the physical.

I've learned to trust that still small voice (actually, sometimes it's really loud, especially when it thinks I'm going to listen to my logical brain instead!). What follows are ideas and examples to inspire your own creativity and ways of enhancing the narrative in your script.

Writing the Eulogy

So many times I've heard celebrants (new and experienced) ask: "How do you write a eulogy for a baby?" Or, "What do you write about a baby born before term?" For creative writing advice on eulogies, see my book *Write That Eulogy*. Many of the ideas in there apply to children of any age, and here's why: *Everyone has a story.* And when it comes to babies, including those who didn't make it Earthside, a lifetime can be lived in every minute for those who are intimately connected.

There are stories everywhere. In every day of the mother's pregnancy, she was taking her baby with her. If you listen to the mother, she'll be able to share with you her wishes, dreams, desires; what she craved and what she was repulsed by. Did she start forming new habits? Did some drop away? Already her baby, from the earliest moments in utero, was making itself known: personality traits were forming.

Fathers can often tell you many things about their baby, too. Maybe they've massaged the mum's growing belly. Perhaps they've sung to their child. Every day they were making memories, and every day their baby was adding something to their lives. Siblings have their stories to share, too, as do grandparents. Listen and listen well.

I believe that we create beautiful ceremony scripts when we use ensouled language. By this, I mean, inhabiting each word and truly feeling it throughout our body.

Ceremonial Space

The space in which we hold ceremony can shape people. As ceremonialists, it may silhouette our craft in many ways. Some places, for example, allow us to connect with the seasons and the gifts of the Earth.

The ceremonial space offers a foothold in which to be held during this time of goodbye.

Nature, and nature alone, may be the décor for our ceremony, or we may add an altar with ceremonial items or a memory table with photos and selected personal mementos. Baskets or urns of flowers, evergreens, or autumn branches may form a centrepiece, or shepherd's crooks with jam jars of wildflowers might create a circle around the ceremonial space. Perhaps there'll be lanterns or candles. Baskets of blankets and cushions, or dolls and teddy bears or toy trains may be placed there.

When working in a crematorium, time restrictions will impose a limit to how creative you are with setting up the space. It's still possible to personalise the room but not necessarily to the degree you can at other locations.

Some venues will allow both the ceremony and funeral tea to be held there, which eliminates the need for travelling across town.

When creating a ceremonial space, consider all the senses at play. Visual is the most obvious one, but reflect on sound, smell and touch too.

♥ A Heart-led Celebrant's Practice ♥

Reflecting on the different ages of childhood, what are some of the ways you can create ceremonial space?

Why might the space feel different for an infant than a teenager, for example?

Botanicals

"In some native languages,
the term for plants translates to
those who take care of us."

- Robin Wall Kimmerer
Braiding Sweetgrass

Although some parents are told by funeral directors not to 'waste money' on flowers for their child's funeral, this is a one-off time in their lives. The choice is theirs. Many families decide that, rather than leave floral displays in the weather outside a crematorium, they'll take them home and dry them. Others press the flowers.

There is no requirement to have flowers on a coffin. Some families have chosen a plant, and others have given small plants, like succulents, flower seeds, spring bulbs, and other funeral favours as a way of remembering their child. Here are some suggestions for using botanicals and other items from nature in ceremonies. May these inspire you to create your own botanic rituals.

Scattering Petals
For example, rose, iris, jasmine, lilac, delphinium.

Daisy Chain
Create a daisy chain for a garland around the shroud of a baby named Daisy.

Lengths of Ivy
Ivy is a symbol of faithfulness; and when we observe the way it grows, attaching itself to something else—twisting, winding and spiralling—we consider it to be a reminder of our bonds with others. Like true love, once ivy makes an attachment it doesn't let go. This was used for a little girl called Ivy (but can be used for any child's funeral). Love transcends time, space and death.

Calendula Cradle
Calendula is one of the most sacred of flowers to ancient Indians. The Romans considered it to have magical powers. Create a cradle of calendula blossoms for a pre-term infant.

Sage for a Stillborn
The herb sage is considered a connection to the divine between our life on Earth and the

higher realms of consciousness. From the Latin, *salveo*, which means to salve or to heal. A salve, as such, it is a sacred herb. Its signature is that of a balm for wounds whether spiritual or physical.

If you're a gardener, you'll know that once sage has been pruned, it renews, and before long is flourishing once again. We can use it in ceremony as a symbol for transformation. It invites the mourner to connect with something far greater than themselves.

- Place branches of sage upon the coffin
- Burn sage around the coffin
- Scatter ground sage around the ceremonial space

Moon Milk for an Infant

Moon Milk offers symbolic nourishment and can be considered a gift from the Divine not only for their newborn infant but the mourners. Moon Milk can be used as a drink, or to sprinkle across the coffin.

- 1 cup plant-based milk
- ½ teaspoon freshly grated nutmeg
- Pinch of cinnamon
- Pinch of cardamom
- Pinch of turmeric

- ¼ teaspoon coconut oil
- Sweetener, as desired

(A lactating mother may wish to infuse this drink with her own milk as a gift to her baby.)

Eucalyptus

The signature of eucalyptus makes it a perfect ally to help alleviate sorrow.

- Carry branches of eucalyptus around the grave three times (either solo, as a celebrant, or with the help of mourners)
- Make a mourning necklace by sewing eucalyptus pods together, and then place on the coffin.

Cosmos Curtain

Cosmos flowers are a symbol of infinity. Create a curtain of cosmos flowers to symbolise the veil between this world and the next. Hang the stems, flowers facing downwards, from a length of string.

Yellow cosmos for a child who laughed a lot.
White as a symbol of innocence.
Pink for a girl.

Rosehip Drink

Rosehips are uplifting, and are often used in rituals and ceremonies for their protective and healing properties. They are a symbol that things can bloom into something beautiful even if we can't see it in the present moment.

Suzie's Banana Bread
Banana is a sacred plant and, spiritually, is considered to release the soul from karma. Some believe that it helps one to connect with the invisible world.

"Suzie loved to help her Mama bake banana bread. It was their Sunday ritual before extended family came to visit." Banana bread is served to mourners as a funerary ritual.

A Blanket of Autumn Leaves
A scattering of colourful Autumn leaves serves as a blanket following a burial. The fallen leaves symbolise change.

A Soft Bed of Moss
At the eco-burial of a stillborn boy, placed on a soft bed of moss, it symbolises softness, connection and mothering.

Starflower Syrup
Starflower (borage) is the flower which symbolises courage and rules the heart. A mouthful (small tumbler) of syrup for each

mourner to acknowledge their bravery during grief. This is passed around to mourners at the start of the ceremony.

Cinnamon Breath
Ask each mourner to help grind cinnamon bark into a powder. When complete, blow a palmful of it into the air in a circle around the ceremonial space.

Apple & Honey Blessing
Mix apple juice and ground cinnamon with a little honey. Use this to sprinkle over the coffin as a protective ritual and to remember the sweetness of the child.

Braided Barley
The parents braid lengths of barley. This is tied to a rock and cast into a body of water. As they do so, they speak their intention for their grief to become one with the wind and water.

A Crown of Carnations
Pink carnations symbolise maternal love.

A small crown is placed on Layla's head following the words of committal.
"Layla Lou, you were the
Princess in our Palace

The beautiful one
who brought meaning to our days
And love to our hearts.
We crown you now with pink carnations."

The Flexibility of Willow
Willow is a beautiful tree to include in ceremonies where you want to bring in the element of water.

Willow Card
Images of weeping willows nearby gravestones were often used on mourning cards. A drawing of a willow can be placed on the coffin or used on an Order of Service.

Willow Wand
A willow wand to offer an invocation or for words of committal:
"Stacy, we now offer your mortal body to the embrace of Mother Earth. With the touch of this wand, we bid you farewell."

Willow Essence
As one of the Bach flower essences, the willow remedy is chosen for people who are feeling bitter, resentful, and unforgiving. The essence, therefore, helps people to release and replace these states with understanding,

compassion and forgiveness. Flower essences are traditionally taken by mouth. This essence can be made into a spray (with spring water) and used to spray amongst the mourners as part of a funeral ritual for forgiveness when a child has suffered death at the hands of others. Walk up the aisle of the chapel, or amongst mourners at a burial site, and spray the essence in silence.

Willow Leaves
A basket full of fresh willow leaves for scattering on top of a woven-willow coffin.

Willow Basket
Willow is associated with the Moon. A basket is passed around mourners for them to select a piece of moonstone to then place on top of the coffin before interment.

Willow-Catkin Binding
A 3-ply cord can be crafted from the wool of catkins and used as a binding. It is a symbol of protection.

Willow-Catkin Blessing
With a branch of catkins, gently touch the feet of the shrouded infant three times following the words of committal.

Willow Dome of Remembrance
Cuttings of willow are planted and woven into a living dome during a memorial ceremony.

Lavender-water Coffin Blessing
- a bowl filled with spring water
- a few drops of lavender essential oil
- bunch of lavender blossom

After the words of committal, dip the bunch of lavender into the water and then sprinkle the water onto the coffin.

Rosemary for Remembrance
Placing rosemary on the coffin is an ancient Welsh funerary ritual. You can place it directly on the coffin, or create a rosemary-water blessing.

> "There's rosemary, that's for remembrance.
> Pray you, love, remember."
> – Shakespeare

Chocolate Blessing
Offer two pieces of chocolate to each mourner. One is for them to eat in remembrance of their sweet memories, and the other is placed on the coffin (as a parting gift) before interment.

Conker Boat

- a cocktail stick
- a little leaf

Make a conker boat, with a message in it, and sail it down the stream! Use the outer shell of a conker, and create a sail with a leaf by using a cocktail stick to attach it to the conker shell.

Bark Stars
Make stars from bark and hang from string.

Love Leaves
- Collect, dry and press your leaves
- Make a wreath
- Make a mobile
- Paint, draw, hole-punch hearts, or write love notes on leaves to the child.

♥ A Heart-led Celebrant's Practice ♥
Choose a botanical from nature that you're particularly drawn to, and write five different ways you could use it in a ritual for a child-bereavement ceremony.

1.

2.

3.

4.

5.

The Five Elements

When a celebrant consciously draws on the five elements in their ceremonial work, it elevates the energetic frequency of everyone present.

Bringing an element into the physical, emotional, mental and spiritual spaces of our work is another way of anchoring ourselves and our clients (and congregation) into an energy field which invites each of us to be fully present in the moment.

It is said that:

Fire glows
Earth grows
Air blows
Water Flows
Spirit knows

Consider each element. Think about the way fire illuminates and energises. It ignites. What inspires you? What *drives* you?

The earth element teaches us about building, healing, nourishing, growing and grounding. What *grounds* you?

If the air element is about breathing, thinking, observing and focus, when left to your own devices, what do you *think* about?

The water element symbolises letting go, flowing, adapting, feeling and cleansing. What has *touched your heart* today?

Fire for desire
Earth for grounding
Air for thinking
Water for feeling

Element work is a large part of my celebrancy practice. When you have a solid understanding of the qualities of each element, you are able to work naturally and authentically in using each one to raise the energy of intention. For deeper exploration, see my book *A Celebrant's Guide: The Five Elements*.

Fire

*"One must never let the fire go out in one's soul,
but keep it burning."*
— Vincent van Gogh

The most obvious representation of fire in our lives is the Sun. Close your eyes and think about how the Sun's rays gently warm your skin. Without fire, we wouldn't be able to cook food, warm ourselves, or have light when the Sun has set.

As an element, we look at themes of creativity, illumination, transformation, passion, strength, brightness, vitality, and movement. It's the *only* element we can't touch without being harmed. To exist, fire needs to consume another element. Despite its power, it can also be extinguished by water, earth and air. It's both a creative and destructive force. There's no ignoring fire. It's captivating and mesmerising.

Some ways we symbolise fire:
- Sun
- Sunlight
- Deserts
- Volcanoes
- Summer
- Masculine
- South
- Sword
- Red, gold, crimson, orange
- Action
- Aries, Leo, Sagittarius
- Drums

The element of fire can be used in obvious ways, such as the lighting of a candle or carrying a lantern.

Fire glows,
it warms,
it radiates.

Candles

A single candle can be lit at the start of the ceremony, and then softly blown out at the end to symbolise the passing of life.

A few candles can be lit at the start of the ceremony with each one representing a different quality of the child.

Burning Bowl

In the case of a death caused by medical mismanagement or a third party, the Burning Bowl ritual is an opportunity to release blame and/or anger, confusion, frustration. Words or sentences with those emotions are written down and then placed in a bowl to burn so that they are not carried around alongside the grief.

Red Marbles

For remembering a fiery child, a collection of red marbles is placed in a large bowl. Each marble is imbued with a blessing from the mourners. The parents run their hands through all the marbles, stirring them around, and remembering all the different ways their child touched other people's lives.

Black Candle

For a Wiccan family, the lighting of a black candle can symbolise the thin veil between this world and the next.

Mango Nectar

Mango, the fruit of the tropics, is a friendly symbolism of the fire element. The nectar can be used as a libation to the earth during an eco burial.

Solar Water

Spring water left in the sunshine all day becomes infused with the energy of the Sun. This water can be utilised in various ways in ceremony:

- Coffin blessing
- Libation
- Stirring water and salt to symbolise tears

Botanicals associated with fire include:
Sunlight lovers: Rosemary, Sunflower and Palm
Spices: Cinnamon, Chili, Pepper, Cloves, Ginger
Red, gold, orange: Marigold, Amaranth, Snapdragon, Calendula, Sagebrush
Fiery: Stinging Nettle, Holly, Cedar, Mace

Sugar and Spice
"What are little girls made of?
Sugar and spice, and everything nice;
That's what little girls are made of."
~ Old Nursery Rhyme

Create a blend of spices and add sugar (or honey, stevia or maple) to taste. Serve in a goblet for the parents to partake.

"With the first sip, remember all the love Jenna brought to your lives."
(*parents sip*)
"With the second sip, be present right here, surrounded by the love of friends and family."
(*parents sip*)
"With the third sip, comes the vow to say Jenna's name freely."
(*parents sip*)

Lantern Walk or Circle
Each person creates a willow lantern. When made, they are placed over tealights (inside a glass jam jar), and a circle of lanterns creates a space where everyone gathers to hear stories about the child.

You'll need:
- tray for the glue
- tissue paper
- PVA glue
- sponge/paint brush
- scissors
- tealight and glass jar
- masking tape
- bamboo or willow

Cut four pieces of willow or bamboo, of equal length and thickness. Tape the corners to make a square, then cut another four pieces to create the height. Tape the ends to the base, and tape them at the top to form a pyramid. If desired, for carrying purposes, make a loop from bending willow and attach it to the top. Alternatively, make lanterns for placing on the ground. Brush each sheet of tissue with diluted PVA glue (half water, half glue). Place it on the lantern, covering all sides. Keep going until you've got each side covered. Leave space at the bottom for your candle.

If making lanterns to carry, you'll need to use LED tealights, and cover most of the base with tissue paper.

If desired, different coloured tissue paper can be used.

♥ A Heart-led Celebrant's Practice ♥
Consider why and when you might bring the element of fire into a child-bereavement ceremony.

Earth

"Forget not that the earth delights
to feel your bare feet
and the winds long to play with your hair."
— Khalil Gibran

When was the last time you hugged a tree or gathered a bouquet of wildflowers, or collected pebbles, or walked barefoot on the grass? Earth grounds us, and is the foothold of our stability.

Correspondences with Earth
- North
- Receptive
- Winter
- Night
- Touch
- Colours: green, black and brown
- Bear, wolf, stag, creatures which burrow, bull, hare
- Taurus, Virgo, Capricorn
- Emerald, jade, tourmaline, onyx, quartz, amethyst
- Saturn, Venus
- Salt, soil, pentacle
- Ivy, nuts, cypress, oak, moss, fern

Rock Painting
Provide mourners with smooth rocks or pebbles and acrylic paints. They can draw an image which will then go into the family's garden. These are symbols of the solidity of the community of friends and extended family who will support them in the years ahead, or in memory of a child who liked to collect pebbles.

Land Art
At the burial site, land art can be created from stones, sticks and other items. This allows the mourners to create a communal gift.

Beach Art
As with land art, a ceremony on the beach can include beach art: seaglass, shells, driftwood, seaweed. This will be washed away with the tide, symbolic of how each of us once again becomes one with the Universal Tide.

Timeline
Use a large roll of white wallpaper and lay it out on a long table. Create a timeline of the child's life, with the minutes, hours, days, weeks, months or years on it. Invite each mourner to put their name at the age when they met the child, or as appropriate to the story. Depending

on the age, you could include significant events in their life and/or photos and pictures to tell the story.

Heart Garland
Wooden hearts with each mourner's name inscribed on them, or with a message of love, are gathered together and strung around the coffin.

Button Bracelet
This ritual offers the family a keepsake. Buttons from their child's clothing are placed into a bowl or basket, and placed at the centre of the ceremonial space. Mourners are invited to choose a button and bestow upon it a prayer, wish or a blessing for the child. They then take turns to thread the button onto a cord. This bracelet can either be worn by various family members, or given a sacred space in the home.

Coloured Ribbons
Each mourner is invited to choose (or bring) a coloured ribbon from a basket. During the reflection music, each one drapes the ribbon over the coffin. A colourful farewell.

Clay Stamps
Have a basket of items from nature: pinecones,

leaves, pebbles. Invite each mourner to press an item into the clay. This nature stamp will be kept as a reminder of the love shared at the funeral.

Mosaic
In memory of the child, a mosaic is created from broken tiles or pieces of pottery. The image might be connected to a favourite hobby.

Amethyst
Amethyst is considered to be a sedative due to its ability to soothe the soul. For help with overwhelming feelings, spray a mist of amethyst-infused spring water around the ceremonial space.

Rose Quartz
Rose quartz is known for opening the heart and releasing grief. Offer pieces to hold or make a rose-quartz spray, or place on/in the coffin.

Mandala
A community mandala is a beautiful expression of creativity and love. Mandala means circle. It can be made from stones, sticks, acorns, rosehips, pine cones, pine needles, flowers, leaves.

Peg Dolls

Using peg dolls, hang a 'clothes line' where memories or photos can be strung up depicting wonderful memories from the child's life.

Pebbles Last Longer Than Flowers

In Hebrew, the word for 'pebble' is *tz'ror* – and it also means 'bond.' There is a tradition of placing a pebble on the grave, rather than flowers, as they last longer.

Earth grows
It grounds
It builds.

♥ A Heart-led Celebrant's Practice ♥

Consider why, how and when you might bring the element of earth into a child-bereavement ceremony.

Air

*"I leave no trace of wings in the air,
but I am glad I have had my flight."*
— Rabindranath Tagore

Maybe you like to fly a kite, ride a hot air balloon or fly a plane. I love to awaken at sunrise and step outside to breathe the fresh air of a new day. The clouds pass across the early morning sky as the birds sing and I lean in close to a flower to breathe in its scent. Back inside, I burn incense. Maybe you start the day by doing deep breathing and yoga asanas or reading a book.

Without air, we'd die. It's essential to life. What is this magical thing that we can't even see, yet is all around us? When we work with the air element, we note how it is connected to freedom, creativity, intuition, communication, travel, intelligence and workings of the mind.

Correspondences
East
Projective energy
Dawn
Springtime
Smell and hearing
Blue, white, yellow
Wand
Wren, eagle, blackbird, hawk, raven, bee
Gemini, Libra, Aquarius
Poppy, lemongrass, dandelion, yarrow, dill, fennel, poplar, frankincense
Sapphire, topaz, smokey quartz
Flute, clarinet, panpipe, whistle

Use the following items in your air rituals:

- bell
- feather
- incense
- chimes
- kite
- bubbles
- knots
- smudging
- dreamcatchers

Blowing Bubbles

Blowing bubbles over the coffin or shroud after the words of committal offers a soft and gentle goodbye. For eco and ethical reasons, I don't use balloons in ceremonies.

Bell Ringing

"With the ringing of this bell,
We wish you safe journey."

I have an assortment of bells in different shapes, styles and sizes. A bell can symbolise crossing the threshold, wishing farewell, time for new beginnings, or to awaken the angels as they greet the child.

Silver Thread

A large ball of silver thread is used. It is first tied around the coffin, then it is passed to the parents to wrap around their wrists several times before passing it to each of the mourners, who also weave it around their wrists. The thread between each person is then cut. The mourners tie the thread around their wrist, a reminder of their interwoven lives. It is then saved as a keepsake (braided into a bookmark, for example). Silver rules the element of air. Air rules relationships and connection.

Dreamcatcher

For a memorial, set up a dreamcatcher-making station so that each person can take one home with them. Talk about the symbolism of them, and the nature of the items used to craft each one.

Seed Bomb

Have a large bowl of wildflower seeds and another bowl of clay. Invite mourners to make seeds bombs that they can take home and plant in memory of the child. Talk about the flowers in the mix and their symbolism.

Fairy Dust

You will need:
- Glitter
- Cornflour
- Lavender blossoms

Using biodegradable glitter (it's made from a cellulose of eucalyptus trees and decomposes naturally), cornflower and chosen ground-up blossoms, mix together and create Fairy Dust. I use this in my naming ceremonies too.

Fairy dust can be:
- strewn around the ceremonial space
- sprinkled over the coffin

- to create a path for the newly bereaved family to walk upon as they recess from the ceremony. A path of new beginnings, accompanied by fairies.
- Can be used to formally name the infant when including a naming ceremony as part of the funeral.

Prayer Flags
- Squares of calico 20cm x 20cm
- Fabric pens

Invite mourners to create images or write a prayer, wish or a blessing for the child. The flags can either be strung up at the ceremony or gathered together for the family to hang up at home or in the garden. Alternatively, it can be used as a garland to wrap around the coffin.

Origami

In Japanese mythology, the wings of the crane carried souls up to heaven. In origami, the folded crane (*Orizuru*) can be used to symbolise sending a message to heaven.

A swan can be made: to contain a message (or ashes) to float down a stream.

Leaf Butterfly
You will need:
- Sticks
- Chalk Pens
- Leaves

Each mourner paints leaves. A leaf is attached either side of a small stick so it looks like a butterfly. These leaf butterflies can have the child's name written on them.

Feathers
Feathers, like bubbles, are beautiful ritual items in child funerals. They lend a softness and subtlety. Try using a white peacock feather.

"What is brought by the wind,
will be carried away by the wind."
— Persian Proverb

♥ **A Heart-led Celebrant's Practice** ♥
Consider why and when you might
bring the element of air into
a child-bereavement ceremony.

Water

"I would love to live like a river flows,
carried by the surprise of its own unfolding."
— John O'Donohue

As I type these words, I'm listening to the rain against the window. Beside me is a glass of water to quench my thirst. Water cleanses, heals, and refreshes us. Energy wise, it represents fluidity and purity.

Correspondences
West
Receptive
Autumn
Dusk
Taste
Blue, green
Chalice, cauldron, cup, bowl
Dolphin, whale, turtle, seal, otter, frog, fish
Cancer, Scorpio, Pisces
Succulents, lily, seaweed, lemon balm, aloe, chamomile
Blue tourmaline, aquamarine, opal, amethyst
Harp, cello, classical guitar

Sail Away With Me

This ritual involves making origami sailboats. These can be made by the congregation of mourners or pre-made. One option is to place a note inside each one of a favourite memory or a small blessing, and another idea is to place ashes in here for a memorial ceremony. If the ceremony is being held alongside a body of water, this ritual is a mindful way of letting go.

Moon Water

Infuse spring water, in a glass, under the energy of the Moon overnight. This water can be used as a libation to the Earth during an eco burial, or sipped to signify healing, or as coffin-blessing water.

Love Tree

You will need:
A few branches of corkscrew willow
Coloured pens
Luggage labels
Stickers, like stars

Each mourner writes a message of love and gratitude to the child, and then places it on the wishing tree. On one side of all the labels are the words: You are loved, (child's name).

Coffin-Blessing Water

Some of the ways I've used water to bless a coffin, are with:

- Lavender
- Iris
- Rosemary
- Salt (to symbolise our tears)
- Honey
- Rose
- Oak leaf
- Acorn
- Pine

When using a plant/flower, I dip the blossom into the water and stir three times before lifting it out and sprinkling the water onto the coffin or shroud.

Collect seashells, seaglass, seaweed, driftwood for a ritual.

Dropping pebbles in water shows the changes that have happened because of that child's presence, and how the ripples will continue long after their funeral day.

♥ A Heart-led Celebrant's Practice ♥
Consider why, how and when you might bring the element of water into a child-bereavement ceremony.

Spirit

*"You are pure space,
uncontaminated by anything.
You are just a mirror reflecting nothing."*
— Osho

A humanist may well skip this section, yet Spirit, the fifth element, is essential in the understanding of the elements. Overlooked by many people, it is the heart, foundation, essence of all that we do. This element, unlike the other four, is not physical. Whether you call it ether or spirit, or the Latin word for 'fifth element', *quintessence,* it is what connects us from the world of physicality to the spiritual or celestial realms. When calling in the directions and elements, I associate Spirit with "As above, so below" and use the colours white or violet and the symbol of a circle. Stars can be symbolised by fire, but are also considered heavenly or otherworldly matter.

*"A great silent space
holds all of nature in its embrace.
It also holds you."*
— Eckhart Tolle

♥ A Heart-led Celebrant's Practice ♥
Consider why, how and when you might bring the element of spirit into a child-bereavement ceremony.

Ensouling Your Craft

There is no question that compassion, awareness and empathy are essential in this role. Are they enough? Maybe. And yet, to ensoul our ceremonies is exactly that: to imbue them with *soul*. To ensoul our craft requires a depth from us that is perhaps not tapped into in day-to-day life. We must allow every word, each action, those moments of body language, our intention, the tone of our voice, and the light within our eyes, to speak on behalf of their loved one, and to speak for the mourners.

We are a channel between life and death, walking the path of the Deathwalker. As Gatekeeper of the Liminal Space we serve as Guardian of the Threshold that the grieving family must walk. We are offering not only a window into the life of their loved one, and then ever so gently closing the curtain (literally or figuratively), but a portal into the dreamworld: the place where each and everyone of us conjures up the life we live.

Our role is to show that every life has meaning. Whether we live to three score years and ten or just weeks in utero, life matters. *Every* life matters. Every life has a purpose even if, through our human eyes, we don't know or understand what the purpose is. The value of a life is not based on longevity.

Grief hurts. It's utterly exhausting, inescapable and relentless. For many, it can be hard to function and think straight. As a celebrant walking into the lives of those who are in grief, especially when they're grieving for a child, our inner well must be full.

Ensouling our craft begins with our daily practices in self-care, self-nurturing and self-love. These are ongoing and require a commitment to one's self if we're going to be of service to others. We are less likely to ensoul our craft if we're spent, exhausted, hungry and in need of care ourselves. To be replenished and revitalised brings luminosity to our heart, to the page, and to the ceremonial space. It is a responsibility to those we serve that we're functioning well.

Making space for our own needs is the number-one job of a child-bereavement celebrant. From there, all other spaces are created and held. And this is the heart and art of ensouling our craft.

May peace be with you. And thank you for all you do and who you are.

"To grieve is to be part of the human experience.
That's the great dare of being human
and being conscious –
to be willing to love something
that's not going to last;
that's a grief-endorsed understanding of life."
— Stephen Jenkinson

About the Author

Veronika Sophia Robinson is an intuitive, empathic Heart-led Celebrant in the north of England. With her husband, Paul, she is co-founder and co-tutor at Heart-led Ceremonies Celebrant Training.

Veronika has been officiating ceremonies since 1995, and also mentors celebrants from around the world, facilitates workshops for celebrants face-to-face and online, and hosts retreats. Veronika is an accredited Infant-Loss Professional; and certified in Self-Harm and Suicide Prevention.

www.veronikarobinson.com
www.starflowerpress.com

About the Artist

Sarah Louise Esau is first and foremost a mother to two home-educated teens. She's married to Sean, who she met in Coogee Bay in Australia, whilst they were both traveling many years ago.

Sarah has over 20-years experience of working with young people both in mainstream and alternative settings. She's a passionate advocate for consent-based, self-directed education, and has published many articles about education, the more recent ones you can find on her blog:
www.unschoolsketchbook.com

Sarah loves to be outdoors walking with her dog, Legend, and observing the changing seasons. She's been a volunteer for mcsuk since 2016, and likes to import, into her drawings, the wonder she experiences when immersed in nature. Sarah has always loved to draw and finds a deep sense of peace when sketching at home with a backdrop of music playing and a cat purring nearby. You can view her illustrations on Instagram: @slesau_art

Starflower Press:
The Celebrant Collection

Other celebrant books by Veronika Robinson:

Write That Eulogy
Funeral Celebrant Ceremony Planner
Wedding Celebrant Ceremony Planner
The Successful Celebrant
The Blessingway
The Discrimination-Free Celebrant: *Unravelling Our Biases and Prejudices*
A Celebrant's Guide: The Five Elements

You can find these books at:
www.starflowerpress.com
www.veronikarobinson.com
Online retailers, good bookshops and libraries.